BARBECUE

BARBECUE

easy recipes • techniques • ingredients

MURDOCH BOOKS

contents

Barbecue basics

Cooking outdoors has come a long way from those early bonfires. This collection of recipes takes you from an easy, mid-week dinner, right through to a Sunday afternoon alfresco feast with friends. You'll find that there's no limit to what can be cooked on a barbecue, from full roasts to seafood and even your favourite desserts.

Barbecues may be a homemade construction consisting of a grill plate balanced over a wood fire, or a state-of-the-art giant with every possible optional extra. Regardless of how yours looks, you'll find recipes in here that not only challenge your idea of what barbecuing is all about, but also fix it in your mind as one of the most fun and tasty ways to prepare food.

Indirect and direct are the main cooking methods when you are using a barbecue. Make sure you set up your barbecue properly to shorten cooking times and ensure perfectly cooked meals.

For direct cooking in a kettle barbecue, start the barbecue and let the briquettes burn for about 45 minutes before you begin cooking. For a medium–hot barbecue, use about 60, for a lower temperature, about 45 briquettes should be enough. If you need to lower the temperature when the fire is already set, just spritz the coals with a light spray of water, but if you want to increase the heat, you will need to add more briquettes and wait for the heat to develop. If you are using a gas or electric barbecue, light the barbecue and let it heat for 10 minutes before cooking.

For indirect cooking in a kettle barbecue, start the barbecue (putting the fuel on each side to leave room for the drip tray) and leave the fire to develop for about 45 minutes. Put a drip tray between the coals and sit the top grill in place. Position the food so that it is over the drip tray and cover it with the lid. Keep the bottom vents open so the heat circulates evenly, and don't open the lid unless it's really necessary — the more often the heat is allowed to escape, the longer your cooking time will be. If you are using a covered gas or electric barbecue, it's best to check the manufacturers' instructions on how to set up your barbecue for indirect cooking. Generally, the outside burners are set to medium–low and the food sits in the middle of the barbecue. This means the heat can circulate around the meat without burning it underneath.

Make sure that the barbecue is clean before lighting it. If possible, clean it out as soon as it is cool enough, brushing or scraping the grill plates and discarding ash and embers. Make sure that the barbecue is in a sheltered position and on a level surface, away from wooden fences, overhanging trees or anything else that may be flammable. Assemble all the equipment you'll need before you start cooking so that you won't have to leave the barbecue unattended. And make it a priority to invest in a small fire extinguisher, in case of emergency.

Brush or spray the barbecue with oil before lighting it in case the oil comes in contact with the flame and flares up. To stop food from sticking, brush it with oil just before cooking it, make sure the grill plate is the correct temperature and don't turn the food until the surface of the food has cooked and 'released' itself naturally from the grill. Food cooked on a grill plate can also be cooked on an open grill provided it is large enough not to fall through the holes. Food cooked on an open grill may also be cooked on a grill plate.

Bring the meat to room temperature before cooking it, but don't leave it sitting at room temperature for more than 20 minutes. Salt meat just before barbecuing as salt will quickly draw moisture out of the meat if it is left. Always soak wooden skewers for an hour before use to prevent them from charring on the grill.

If you wish to use the marinade to baste, you must boil it, then let it simmer for at least 5 minutes before basting so that any bacteria from the raw meat are not transferred to the cooked meat. If you are basting the food with a sugary glaze, apply it only during the last 10 minutes of cooking, as it will tend to burn on the barbecue grill.

main meals

Food never tastes better than when it is cooked outdoors. Whether you use traditional wood, or modern briquettes or gas, you'll still get that sought-after, flame-grilled flavour. Many cultures in the world have a tradition of gathering for a meal cooked in this way. It's a ritual that transforms ordinary food into a delicious feast, delicately smoked or bursting with robust flavours and juices.

Venture beyond the confines of the kitchen, bring your barbecue out of weekday exile and get it going with fantastic everyday dinners, or celebrate a big event with surprisingly little effort. We've drawn on every corner of the world to bring you meals from Asia, North Africa, Europe, the Americas and Australia, so you can follow the recipes as they stand or pick and mix a Moroccan roast, an Italian salad and finish with an Asian-inspired dessert. Best of all, gather your friends and family around for one of the most important of occasions — sharing good food and good company.

Many recipes can be prepared ahead, with meat or fish, for example, being left to marinate in a mixture of flavoursome and aromatic ingredients. It's a quick and easy way to add maximum flavour to food with minimum effort. Keep your kitchen shelves well stocked with dried herbs and spices and variety will always be within your reach.

Steak sandwich with balsamic onions

SERVES 4

sour cream	125 g (5 oz/½ cup)
sun-dried tomatoes	40 g (1½ oz/¼ cup), well drained and finely chopped
garlic cloves	3, crushed
basil leaves	2 tablespoons finely chopped
lemon juice	2 teaspoons
red onions	2
olive oil	2 tablespoons
balsamic vinegar	2 tablespoons
soft brown sugar	1 tablespoon
sourdough bread	8 large slices
fillet steak	400 g (14 oz) piece, cut into 1 cm (½ inch) thick slices
baby rocket (arugula) leaves	4 handfuls, rinsed and well drained

Preheat the barbecue to medium–high direct heat. Mix the sour cream, sun-dried tomatoes, garlic, basil and lemon juice in a small bowl and season the mixture to taste.

Thinly slice the onions, separate the rings and toss them with 1 tablespoon of the olive oil. Spread the onion across the flat grill plate and cook it for 10 minutes, or until it is softened and starting to brown, then gather the rings into a pile and pour the combined balsamic vinegar and sugar over them. Turn the onion so that it is well coated in the balsamic mixture, then spread it out a little and cook for a few more minutes, or until it is slightly glazed. Remove the onion from the barbecue and toast the bread on the chargrill plate for 30 seconds on each side, or until grill marks appear.

Brush the steaks with a little olive oil and season with salt and freshly ground black pepper. Chargrill them for 1 minute on each side for medium–rare, or 2 minutes for well done.

To make each sandwich, put a piece of steak on a slice of toasted bread and top with the onion, a dollop of the sour cream mixture and some rocket leaves. Finish with a second piece of toast and serve immediately.

Note Suitable for any type of barbecue.

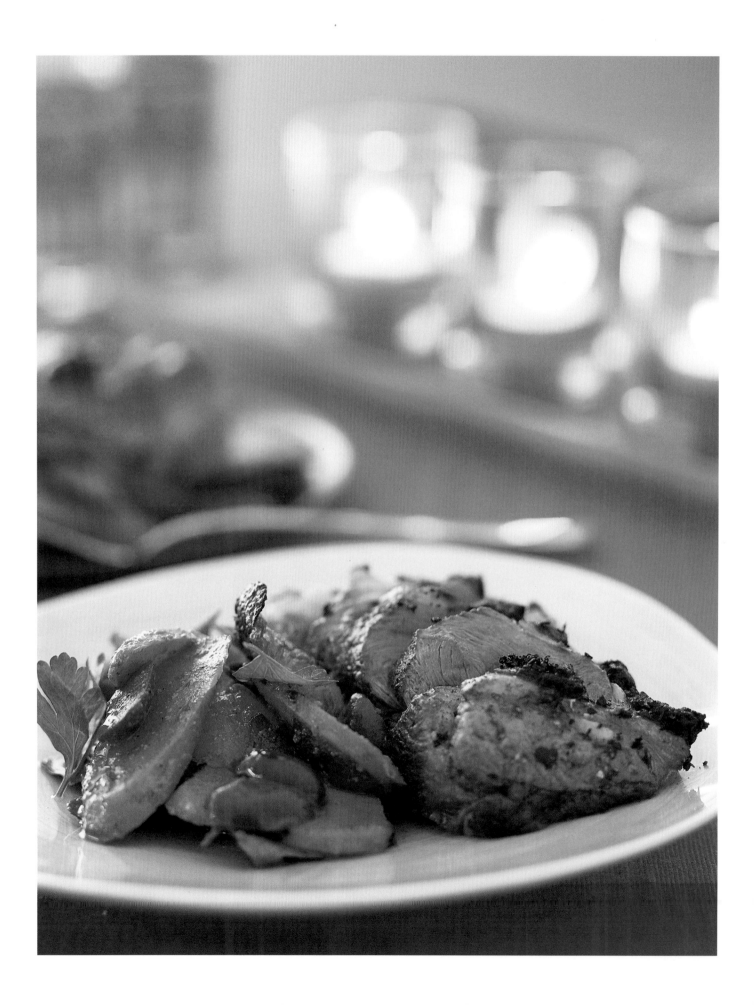

Lamb with Moroccan spiced carrot salad   SERVES 4

lamb marinade

flat-leaf (Italian) parsley	1 large handful, finely chopped
coriander (cilantro) leaves	2 handfuls, finely chopped
garlic cloves	4 crushed
paprika	1 tablespoon
dried thyme	1 teaspoon
olive oil	125 ml (4 fl oz/^{1}/$_2$ cup)
lemon juice	60 ml (2 fl oz/^{1}/$_4$ cup)
ground cumin	2 teaspoons
lamb rumps or pieces of tenderloin	4 x 250 g (9 oz), trimmed

carrot salad

carrots	4, peeled, trimmed and halved on the diagonal
olive oil	80 ml (3 fl oz/^{1}/$_3$ cup)
ground cumin	2 teaspoons
Kalamata olives	95 g (3 oz/^{1}/$_2$ cup), pitted and halved lengthways
flat-leaf (Italian) parsley	1 handful
harissa	1 teaspoon
extra virgin olive oil	2 tablespoons
red wine vinegar	1 tablespoon

Mix the parsley, coriander, garlic, paprika, thyme, olive oil, lemon juice and 1^1/$_2$ teaspoons cumin together in a non-metallic dish. Score diagonal lines in the fat on the lamb pieces with a sharp knife, then put them in the marinade, turning so they are evenly coated. Cover and refrigerate the lamb for at least 2 hours or overnight.

To make the spiced carrot salad, preheat the flat plate to low. Bring a saucepan of salted water to the boil and blanch the carrots for 3 minutes, or until they just begin to soften. Drain, pat dry with paper towels, then toss them with 2 tablespoons of the olive oil and 1 teaspoon of the cumin. Cook the carrots for 25 minutes, turning them once so they are cooked through and golden all over.

While the carrots are still warm, cut them into thin diagonal slices and toss with the olives and parsley. Mix the harissa with 1 tablespoon of water, add the extra virgin olive oil, red wine vinegar, remaining olive oil and remaining cumin, and whisk it together. Pour the dressing over the salad and season to taste with salt and pepper.

Increase the heat under the flat plate to medium direct heat. Season the lamb with white pepper, the remaining cumin and some salt. Cook the rumps fat side up for 3 minutes and then cook the other side for 2–3 minutes, making sure the fat is well cooked. Take the lamb off the barbecue as soon as it is done, cover it with foil and put it aside to rest for about 5 minutes before carving. Serve it with the warm carrot salad.

Note Suitable for a flat or ridged grill plate.

Lemon and thyme roasted chicken

chicken	1 x 1.8 kg (4 lb)
garlic cloves	12, unpeeled
lemon thyme	10 sprigs
lemon	1, halved
olive oil	1 tablespoon
zucchini (courgettes)	8 small, halved lengthways
flat-leaf (Italian) parsley	2 tablespoons chopped
plain (all-purpose) flour	1 tablespoon
chicken stock	250 ml (9 fl oz/1 cup)

Remove the giblets and any large fat deposits from inside the chicken, then pat it dry inside and out with paper towels. Season the cavity with salt and pepper and stuff it with the unpeeled garlic cloves and the sprigs of thyme. Rub the skin with the cut lemon, making sure that it is evenly coated all over, then brush it with 2 teaspoons of the oil and season with salt and black pepper.

Preheat a kettle or covered barbecue to medium indirect heat, with a drip tray underneath the grill. Position the chicken on the barbecue directly over the drip tray, close the hood and roast the chicken for 1 hour, or until the juices run clear when it is pierced with a skewer between the thigh and the body.

When the chicken has been cooking for 40 minutes, toss the zucchini with the remaining olive oil and season it with salt and black pepper. Arrange the zucchini on the grill around the chicken, re-cover the kettle and cook the chicken and the zucchini for 20–25 minutes, or until the zucchini is tender, but not soggy. Put the zucchini in a serving dish and sprinkle it with the parsley. When the chicken is ready, remove it from the barbecue, cover it loosely with foil and leave it to rest for 10 minutes. Remove the garlic from the chicken cavity but do not peel the cloves.

If you would like gravy with the chicken, pour the contents of the drip tray into a container and skim off as much fat as possible. Tip the remaining juices into a saucepan, add the flour and stir well to combine. Cook the gravy over medium heat for 3–4 minutes, or until it has thickened, then add the chicken stock and any juices that have been released from the chicken while it was resting. Bring the gravy to the boil, then reduce the heat and simmer it for 3–4 minutes. Season the gravy to taste, strain it into a jug and serve it with the chicken, garlic and zucchini.

Note Suitable for a covered barbecue.

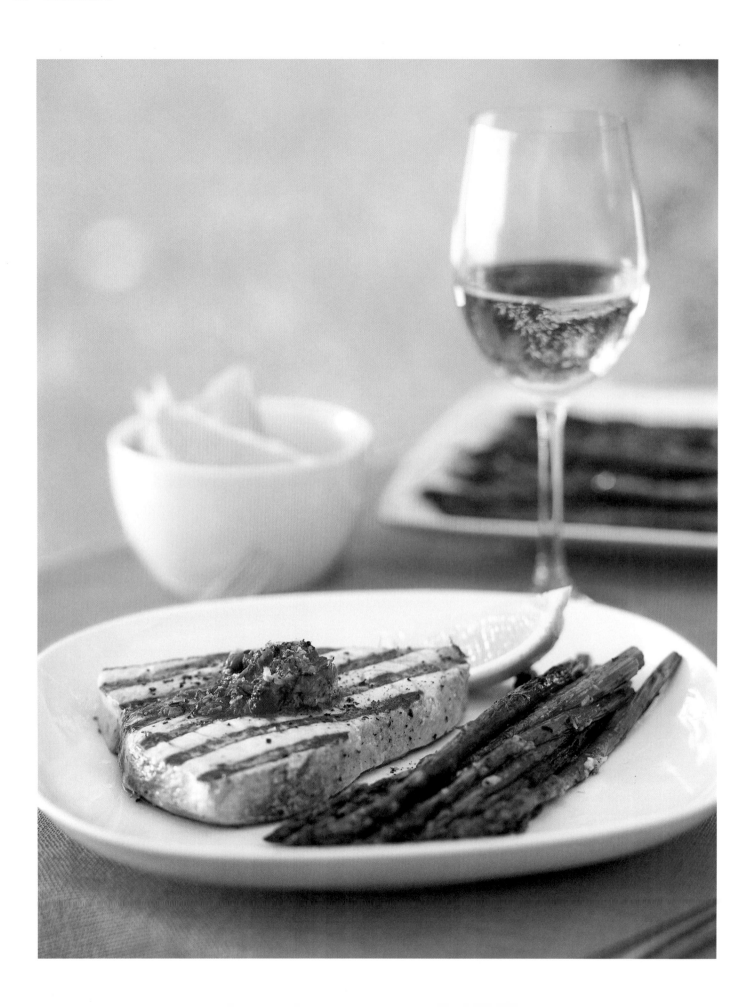

Swordfish with tomato butter

butter	100 g (4 oz), softened
semi-dried (sun-blushed) tomatoes	50 g (2 oz/⅓ cup), finely chopped
baby capers in brine	2 tablespoons, drained and crushed
shredded basil leaves	1½ tablespoons
garlic cloves	4, crushed
extra virgin olive oil	60 ml (2 fl oz/¼ cup)
slender asparagus spears	300 g (11 oz), trimmed
swordfish steaks	4

Put the butter in a bowl with the tomato, capers, basil and two cloves of crushed garlic, and mash it all together. Shape the flavoured butter into a log, then wrap it in baking paper and twist the ends to close them off. Refrigerate the butter until firm, then cut it into 1 cm (½ inch) slices and leave it, covered, at room temperature until ready to use.

Mix 2 tablespoons of the oil and the remaining garlic in a small bowl. Toss the asparagus spears with the oil until they are well coated, season them with salt and pepper, and leave for 30 minutes.

Preheat the ridged grill plate to high direct heat. Brush the swordfish steaks with the remaining oil and cook them for 2–3 minutes on each side or until they are just cooked through. Don't overcook the fish as residual heat will continue to cook the meat after it has been removed from the barbecue. Put a piece of the tomato butter on top of each steak as soon as it comes off the barbecue and season to taste. Cook the asparagus on the chargrill plate, turning it regularly, for 2–3 minutes, or until it is just tender. Serve the asparagus immediately with the fish.

Note Suitable for any barbecue.

Bruschetta with mushrooms

SERVES 6

field mushrooms	5 small, quartered
red onion	1, halved and thinly sliced
olive oil	170 ml (6 fl oz/²⁄₃ cup)
garlic cloves	3, crushed
oregano leaves	1½ tablespoons chopped
crème fraîche	60 g (2 oz/¼ cup)
Dijon mustard	1 teaspoon
ciabatta bread	1 loaf
olive oil	60 ml (2 fl oz/¼ cup), extra
garlic clove	1 large, extra, peeled and halved
oregano leaves	small handful
mixed lettuce leaves	6 handfuls
extra virgin olive oil	2 tablespoons
lemon juice	1 tablespoon

Put the mushrooms and onion in separate bowls and season with salt and pepper. Whisk together the oil, crushed garlic and oregano and pour two-thirds of the mixture over the mushrooms and the rest over the onion. Toss the vegetables so that they are well coated in the marinade, then cover and refrigerate both of the bowls for 30 minutes. Mix the crème fraîche and mustard together, then refrigerate it until you are ready to use it.

Heat the barbecue to medium direct heat. Cut the bread into twelve 1 cm (½ inch) thick slices and brush both sides of each slice with the extra oil. Toast the bread on the chargrill plate for 1–2 minutes on each side or until it is golden and lightly charred, then rub one side of each slice with the cut side of the garlic clove. Cook the onion on the flat plate, tossing it gently, for 2–3 minutes or until soft and golden. Next, cook the mushrooms on the flat plate for 2 minutes on each side or until cooked through, then toss the onion and mushrooms together.

Arrange the mushrooms and onion on the garlic-rubbed side of the bread slices and top with a teaspoon of the mustard crème fraîche. Garnish each piece with oregano leaves and season with salt and pepper. Toss the lettuce leaves with the extra virgin olive oil and lemon juice, and serve with the bruschetta.

Note Suitable for a flat or ridged grill plate.

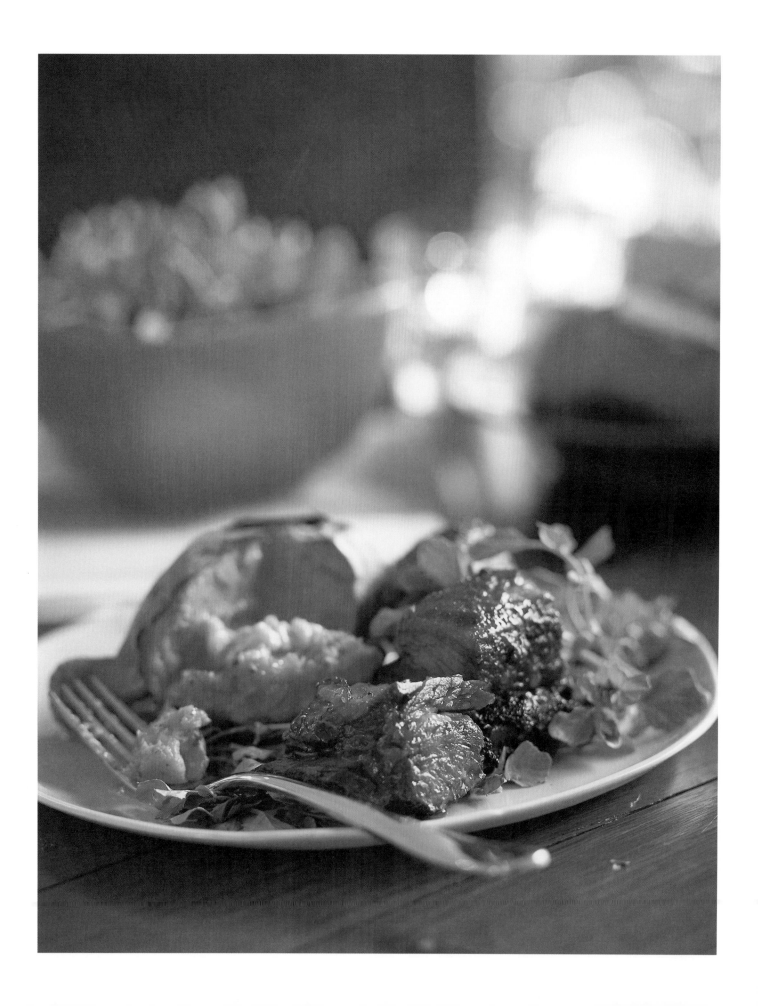

Bourbon beef ribs with sweet potato

SERVES 4–6

marinade

chilli powder	¼ teaspoon
chilli flakes	½ teaspoon
celery salt	½ teaspoon
cayenne pepper	⅛ teaspoon
cider vinegar	500 ml (17 fl oz/2 cups)
lemon juice	60 ml (2 fl oz/¼ cup)
garlic cloves	6, crushed
paprika	1 tablespoon
garlic powder	1 teaspoon
onion powder	1 teaspoon
Worcestershire sauce	125 ml (4 fl oz/½ cup)
beef loin ribs (see Notes)	3 kg (6 lb 8 oz)

sweet potatoes

butter	60 g (2 oz), softened
maple syrup	1 tablespoon
pecan nuts	1 tablespoon chopped
garlic salt	½ teaspoon
sweet potatoes	4 x 200 g (7 oz)

barbecue sauce

tomato sauce	500 ml (17 fl oz/2 cups)
soft brown sugar	55 g (2 oz/¼ cup)
bourbon	80 ml (3 fl oz/⅓ cup)
Dijon mustard	60 g (2 oz/¼ cup)
Tabasco sauce	1½ tablespoons
paprika	2 teaspoons
garlic powder	1 teaspoon
onion powder	1 teaspoon
Worcestershire sauce	1½ tablespoons

Combine the marinade ingredients with ¼ teaspoon pepper and ¼ teaspoon salt, and rub the marinade all over the ribs. Put the ribs in a non-metallic bowl, cover them and refrigerate overnight.

Mash together the butter, maple syrup, pecans, garlic salt and some black pepper, and cover until you are ready to dish up. Put all of the barbecue sauce ingredients in a saucepan and stir them together. Simmer the sauce over low heat for 15 minutes, or until the mixture has thickened, stirring constantly. Take care while stirring the sauce as it might splatter a bit.

Preheat a kettle or covered barbecue to very low indirect heat. Remove the ribs from the marinade and baste them all over with the barbecue sauce. Cook them on the flat plate for 3 hours, or until they are very tender, turning and basting them every 30 minutes. Arrange the whole sweet potatoes on a lightly greased baking tray and add them to the barbecue 45 minutes before the ribs have finished cooking. Remove the ribs and sweet potatoes from the barbecue, slice each sweet potato down the middle and top each with some of the flavoured butter. Cut between the ribs to separate them and serve the ribs with the sweet potatoes.

Notes Beef loin ribs are also known as beef shortribs. Make sure the barbecue temperature remains low and constant because, if the heat is too high, the ribs will burn before they become tender. Suitable for a covered barbecue.

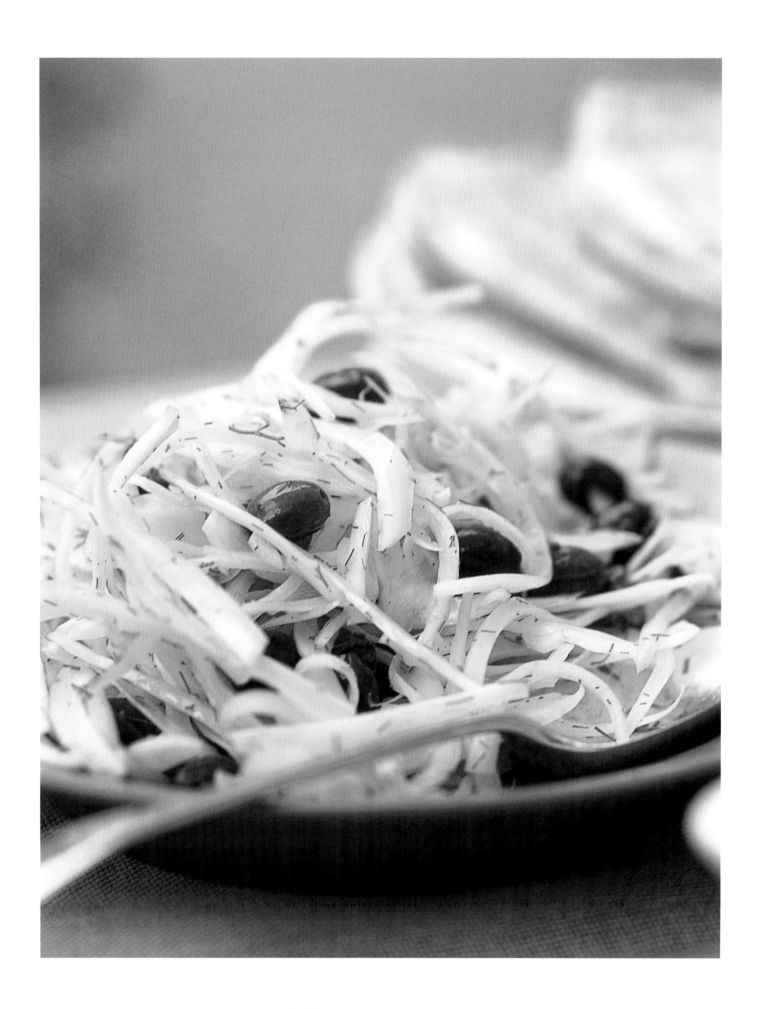

three ways with salad

Salads can be light, complementing a main course, or they can served as an appetite-teasing starter. They can also be substantial meals in their own right, based around generous servings of meat, tofu or seafood. And, they can be dressed with the simplest dash of oil and vinegar, homemade mayonnaise or special vinaigrettes. The recipes given here showcase vegetables and herbs and are all refreshing and robust in flavours.

FENNEL SALAD

Trim 2 large fennel bulbs, reserving the fronds, and discard the tough outer layers. Using a very sharp knife, slice the fennel bulbs lengthways as thinly as possible and put it in a bowl of very cold water with 1 tablespoon lemon juice. Just before you are ready to serve, drain the fennel well, pat it dry with paper towels and toss it in a bowl with 1 tablespoon olive oil and 2 teaspoons red wine vinegar. Finely chop the reserved fronds, add them to the fennel with 150 g (5 oz) pitted Niçoise olives and then season to taste with freshly ground black pepper. Serves 4

TABBOULEH

Cover 130 g (5 oz/³/4 cup) burghul (bulgar) with 500 ml (17 fl oz/2 cups) water and leave it to soak for 1¹/2 hours. Drain the burghul, squeezing out any excess water, and spread it out across a clean tea towel (dish towel) for 30 minutes to dry. Cut 3 ripe tomatoes in half, squeeze the halves gently to remove any excess seeds and cut the flesh into 5 mm (¹/4 inch) cubes. Cut 1 telegraph (long) cucumber in half lengthways, remove the seeds and cut the flesh into 5 mm (¹/4 inch) cubes. Whisk together 80 ml (3 fl oz/¹/3 cup) lemon juice and 1¹/2 teaspoons of salt until they are well combined. Season the dressing with pepper, then slowly whisk in 80 ml (3 fl oz/¹/3 cup) extra virgin olive oil. Put the burghul in a large bowl and add the tomato, cucumber, 4 sliced spring onions (scallions), 120 g (4 oz/1 bunch) chopped flat-leaf (Italian) parsley and 4 tablespoons chopped mint. Toss the dressing with the tabbouleh, then cover and refrigerate. Serves 4

CUCUMBER SALAD

Peel 1 telegraph (long) cucumber, cut it in half lengthways, remove the seeds and cut it into 5 mm (¹/4 inch) slices. Finely chop 1 small red chilli, removing the seeds. Put 1 tablespoon sugar and 60 ml (2 fl oz/¹/4 cup) lime juice in a large bowl and stir until the sugar has dissolved. Add 1 tablespoon fish sauce. Toss the cucumber, chilli, 1 finely sliced Asian shallot and 1 handful coriander (cilantro) leaves through the dressing, cover and refrigerate for 15 minutes. Just before serving, cut 75 g (3 oz) snow pea shoots in half and stir them through the salad. Serves 4

fennel salad

Lamb kofta with baba ganouj

kofta

red onion	1, finely chopped
flat-leaf (Italian) parsley	2 large handfuls, chopped
coriander (cilantro) leaves	2 large handfuls, chopped
mint leaves	1 large handful, chopped
paprika	1 tablespoon
ground cumin	1 tablespoon
allspice	1½ teaspoons
ground ginger	½ teaspoon
chilli flakes	½ teaspoon
minced (ground) lamb	1.2 kg (2 lb 11 oz)
soda water	60 ml (2 fl oz/¼ cup)

baba ganouj

eggplants (aubergines)	2 (820 g/1 lb 13 oz)
garlic cloves	2, finely chopped
ground cumin	¼ teaspoon
lemon juice	60 ml (2 fl oz/¼ cup)
tahini	2–2½ tablespoons
olive oil	60 ml (2 fl oz/¼ cup)

flat-leaf (Italian) parsley	1 tablespoon chopped
sumac	½ teaspoon
Kalamata olives	200 g (7 oz/1 cup)
olive oil	for brushing
pitta bread	4 pieces
tabbouleh	to serve (page 27)

To make the kofta, put the onion, herbs and spices in a food processor and blend until combined. Season the mixture with 2 teaspoons salt and some freshly ground black pepper, then add the minced lamb to the food processor and get the motor going again. Add the soda water in a thin stream until the mixture forms a smooth paste, then cover and refrigerate for at least 2 hours, or overnight.

To make the baba ganouj, preheat a covered barbecue chargrill plate to medium–high. Prick the eggplants a few times with a fork and cook, covered, for 20 minutes, or until they are soft and wrinkled, turning halfway through the cooking time. Put the eggplants in a colander and leave them for 30 minutes to allow any bitter juices to drain, then peel and discard the skin and roughly chop the flesh. Put the eggplant in a food processor with the garlic, cumin, lemon juice, tahini and olive oil and process for 30 seconds, or until smooth and creamy. Season to taste with salt, then cover and refrigerate. Sprinkle the baba ganouj with the parsley and sumac before serving.

Soak four wooden skewers in cold water for 1 hour. Divide the lamb mixture into 12 portions and mould each portion into a torpedo shape, using damp hands to stop the meat sticking, then cover and refrigerate the kofta. Thread the olives onto the soaked skewers.

When you're ready to cook the kofta, preheat the flat grill plate to medium–high direct heat. Brush the kofta lightly with olive oil and cook, turning frequently, for 10–12 minutes, or until evenly browned and cooked through. When they are nearly cooked, add the olives to the barbecue for 1–2 minutes. Serve the kofta immediately with pitta bread, the baba ganouj, olives and some tabbouleh.

Note Suitable for a covered barbecue.

Portuguese spatchcock

red onion	1, chopped
garlic cloves	6, chopped
lemon zest	3 teaspoons grated
chilli flakes	2 teaspoons
paprika	1½ teaspoons
oil	60 ml (2 fl oz/¼ cup)
red wine vinegar	60 ml (2 fl oz/¼ cup)
spatchcocks (poussin)	4 x 500 g (1 lb 2 oz)
flat-leaf (Italian) parsley	3 tablespoons chopped
lemon halves	to serve

Put the onion, garlic, lemon zest, chilli flakes, paprika, oil and vinegar in a food processor and blend them to a smooth paste.

Cut each of the spatchcocks down the backbone with sharp kitchen scissors and press down on the breastbone to flatten it out. Score the flesh and brush it with the spice mixture, then put the spatchcocks in a non-metallic dish, cover and refrigerate overnight.

Preheat the chargrill plate to low–medium direct heat. Grill the spatchcocks for 10 minutes on each side, or until they are cooked through (test by piercing the thigh with a skewer — if the juices run clear, they are ready), then sprinkle them with parsley and serve with the lemon halves.

Notes Try grilling the lemon halves for a bit of extra flavour. Suitable for any type of barbecue.

Stuffed pork chops with spring onions

SERVES 6

dry sherry	2 tablespoons
figs	4 dried dessert
butter	1 tablespoon
olive oil	60 ml (2 fl oz/¼ cup)
onion	1 small, finely diced
garlic cloves	2, crushed
Granny Smith apple	1 large, peeled, cored and grated
slivered almonds	2 tablespoons lightly toasted
sage leaves	1 tablespoon finely chopped
pork loin chops	6 large (250 g/9 oz each) on the bone
bulb spring onions (scallions)	16 large, green parts removed, halved

Bring the sherry and 1 tablespoon of water to the boil in a small saucepan. Soak the figs in the hot sherry mixture for 20 minutes, then slice them finely and reserve the soaking liquid to use later.

Heat the butter and 1 tablespoon of olive oil in a frying pan, add the onion and garlic, and cook over low heat for 5 minutes or until they are softened. Add the grated apple, figs and sherry liquid, and simmer for a further 5 minutes, or until the apple has softened and most of the liquid has evaporated. Remove the pan from the heat and stir in the almonds and sage, then season well and allow the mixture to cool.

Trim the pork chops of any excess fat and make an incision into the middle of the chop from the side. Be careful — you only want to make a pocket in the flesh and not cut right through. Fill the pocket with the apple and fig stuffing, pushing it well into the cavity so that none is spilling out; you should fit about 1½ tablespoons of filling in each chop. Brush the chops all over with 1 tablespoon of the olive oil, and season with salt and freshly ground black pepper. Toss the spring onion with the remaining oil, and season it well.

Heat the chargrill plate to medium direct heat. Cook the pork chops for 8 minutes on each side, or until the outside is slightly charred and the meat is cooked through. While the chops are cooking, add the spring onions to the chargrill plate and cook them for 10 minutes, or until they are softened. Serve the chops and spring onions as soon as they come off the barbecue.

Note Suitable for a flat or ridged grill plate.

Miso-glazed salmon and eggplant salad   SERVES 4

sesame seeds	65 g (2 oz/heaped ⅓ cup), lightly toasted
white miso	70 g (3 oz/¼ cup)
sake	1 tablespoon
mirin	1 tablespoon
sugar	1 tablespoon
dashi stock	125 ml (4 fl oz/½ cup)
eggplant (aube1rgine)	1 large, cut into 1 cm (½ inch) rounds
garlic cloves	2, crushed
olive oil	60 ml (2 fl oz/¼ cup)
dark soy sauce	2 teaspoons
sugar	1 teaspoon, extra
ginger	1 teaspoon grated
snow pea shoots	150 g (5 oz)
daikon	400 g (14 oz), very thinly sliced
salmon fillets	4, skin removed

To make the miso glaze, put the sesame seeds in a spice grinder or mortar and pestle and grind them until they have a rough, flaky texture. Whisk the miso, sake, mirin, sugar and half the dashi stock together until smooth and stir in half of the crushed sesame seeds.

Put the eggplant rounds in a large bowl with the combined garlic and oil, season them with salt and pepper and toss until the rounds are well coated.

To make the dressing, whisk together the soy sauce, extra dashi stock and sugar, ginger and remaining crushed sesame seeds. Put the snow pea shoots and daikon in a large bowl, add the soy dressing and toss them until they are well combined. Cover the bowl and refrigerate until needed.

Heat the barbecue to medium–high direct heat. Cook the eggplant on the chargrill plate for 3–4 minutes on each side, or until it has softened, then allow it to cool slightly and cut it into quarters. Brush both sides of each salmon fillet with the miso glaze and cook them on the flat plate for 2 minutes each side, or until they are almost cooked through, brushing with the glaze while they are cooking. Flake the fillets with a fork and toss them through the salad with the eggplant slices. Season and serve the salad straight away.

Note Suitable for any type of barbecue.

Roast beef with barbecue sauce

paprika	2 tablespoons
onion powder	1 tablespoon
garlic powder	1 tablespoon
sugar	2 teaspoons
chilli powder	1 teaspoon
oil	60 ml (2 fl oz/¼ cup)
beef fillet	1 x 1.5 kg (3 lb 5 oz) piece

barbecue sauce

oil	2 tablespoons
onion	1 small, finely chopped
garlic cloves	4, crushed
chilli flakes	½ teaspoon
paprika	1 tablespoon
smoked paprika	½ teaspoon
tomato sauce	375 ml (13 fl oz/1½ cups)
beer	125 ml (4 fl oz/½ cup)
cider vinegar	60 ml (2 fl oz/¼ cup)
soft brown sugar	80 ml (3 fl oz/⅓ cup)
Dijon mustard	2 tablespoons
Worcestershire sauce	80 ml (3 fl oz/⅓ cup)

Mix the paprika, onion powder, garlic powder, sugar, chilli powder, 2 teaspoons ground black pepper, 2 teaspoons salt and the oil in a small bowl. Rub the mixture all over the beef fillet, then cover it with plastic wrap and refrigerate overnight.

To make the barbecue sauce, put the oil in a small saucepan over medium heat, add the onion, garlic and chilli flakes, and cook them for 5 minutes or until the onion is soft. Add the remaining ingredients and 60 ml (2 fl oz/¼ cup) water, and let the sauce simmer over low heat for 20 minutes, or until it is slightly thickened. Season well and let it cool.

Preheat a kettle or covered barbecue to medium indirect heat. Put the beef fillet in the middle of the hot barbecue and cook, covered, for 40 minutes for rare beef. If you would like medium beef, leave it to roast for another 10 minutes.

Brush the barbecue sauce all over the beef and cook, covered, for another 10 minutes. Remove the beef from the barbecue, cover it loosely with foil and let it rest for 10 minutes before carving and serving it with the remaining barbecue sauce.

Note Suitable for a covered barbecue.

Chicken tikka with garlic naan

SERVES 4

tikka paste	100 g (4 oz/^{1}/$_3$ cup)
Greek-style plain yoghurt	60 g (2 oz/^{1}/$_4$ cup)
boneless, skinless chicken breasts	600 g (1 lb 5 oz), cut into 3 cm (1^1/$_4$ inch) cubes
red onions	2 small, quartered
oil	for brushing
coriander (cilantro) leaves	2 tablespoons chopped

apple raita

green apple	1, grated
lemon juice	2 teaspoons
sour cream	60 g (2 oz/^{1}/$_4$ cup)
mint leaves	3 tablespoons chopped

garlic naan

garlic clove	1, crushed
butter	2 tablespoons, softened
naan bread	4 plain

Stir the tikka paste and yoghurt, together, add the chicken and turn it until evenly coated in the tikka mixture. Cover with plastic wrap and refrigerate it for 4 hours or overnight.

To make the raita, put the apple, lemon juice, sour cream and mint in a small bowl and stir together. Cover and refrigerate it until you are ready to dish up. Mash the crushed garlic and butter together and brush one side of each piece of naan with about 2 teaspoons of garlic butter.

Soak four wooden skewers in cold water for 1 hour and preheat the barbecue to low–medium direct heat. Thread the chicken and onion pieces onto the skewers and cook them on the flat plate for 5–6 minutes on each side, turning once. A little before the chicken is ready, lightly brush the chargrill plate with some oil. Grill the naan, buttered side down, for 1–2 minutes, or until the bread is golden and marked. Turn it and grill for 1 minute on the other side.

Sprinkle the skewers with the chopped coriander and serve them with the garlic naan and apple raita.

Note Suitable for any type of barbecue.

Chargrilled cauliflower salad with tahini — SERVES 4

tahini dressing	
tahini	65 g (2 oz/¼ cup)
garlic clove	1, crushed
rice vinegar	60 ml (2 fl oz/¼ cup)
oil	1 tablespoon
sesame oil	¼ teaspoon
lemon juice	1 teaspoon
sesame seeds	2 teaspoons, toasted
flat-leaf (Italian) parsley	1 tablespoon finely chopped
garlic clove	½ small, finely chopped
lemon zest	½ teaspoon finely grated
cauliflower	1 (about 1.8 kg/4 lb)
oil	2 tablespoons
baby Cos (romaine) lettuces	2, washed and drained
watercress leaves	50 g (1¾ oz/1⅔ cups), washed and drained

To make the dressing, whisk the tahini, garlic, rice vinegar, oils, lemon juice and 1 tablespoon of water together and season.

Stir the sesame seeds, parsley, garlic and lemon zest together.

Divide the cauliflower into large florets and cut each floret into 1 cm (½ inch) thick slices, then brush with oil and season well. Preheat the chargrill plate to medium direct heat and chargrill the cauliflower pieces for 6–8 minutes, or until they are cooked and golden on both sides.

Arrange the Cos leaves and watercress on a serving dish and top them with the chargrilled cauliflower slices. Drizzle the tahini dressing over the cauliflower, sprinkle it with the sesame seed mixture and serve it while it is still piping hot.

Note Suitable for a flat or ridged grill plate.

Roast lamb with ratatouille

leg of lamb	1 x 2.5 kg (5 lb 8 oz)
garlic cloves	6, peeled
rosemary leaves	2 tablespoons
olive oil	1 tablespoon

ratatouille

garlic	1 bulb
olive oil	80 ml (3 fl oz/$\frac{1}{3}$ cup)
Roma (plum) tomatoes	6, halved lengthways
baby eggplants (aubergines)	4, cut into 1 cm ($\frac{1}{2}$ inch) pieces on the diagonal
zucchini (courgettes)	3, cut into 1 cm ($\frac{1}{2}$ inch) pieces on the diagonal
red capsicums (peppers)	2, seeded and cut into wedges
red onions	2, cut into 1 cm ($\frac{1}{2}$ inch) thick rounds
balsamic vinegar	2 tablespoons

Make 12 small incisions in the fleshy parts of the lamb. Cut the garlic cloves in half lengthways, and push them into the incisions with the rosemary leaves. Rub the lamb with the oil and season it liberally with salt and pepper. Preheat a kettle or covered barbecue to medium indirect heat, put the lamb in the middle of the barbecue, replace the lid, and let it roast for 1 hour 30 minutes.

Meanwhile, to make the ratatouille, trim the top of the garlic bulb so that the cloves are just exposed, drizzle 1 teaspoon of olive oil over the cut end and wrap the bulb in foil. Put the garlic in the barbecue with the lamb for 30 minutes, or until it has softened. Brush the vegetables with 2 tablespoons of olive oil and add them to the barbecue when the garlic has been cooking for about 15 minutes. Cook the vegetables for 5–8 minutes on each side, or until they are marked and cooked through, then put them in a large bowl. Squeeze the garlic cloves out of their skins and add them to the vegetables. Mix the balsamic vinegar and remaining olive oil together, gently toss it with the ratatouille and season well.

When the lamb is ready, remove it from the barbecue and let it rest, covered, for 10 minutes before carving and serving it with the ratatouille and any juices that have been released while it rested.

Note Suitable for a covered barbecue.

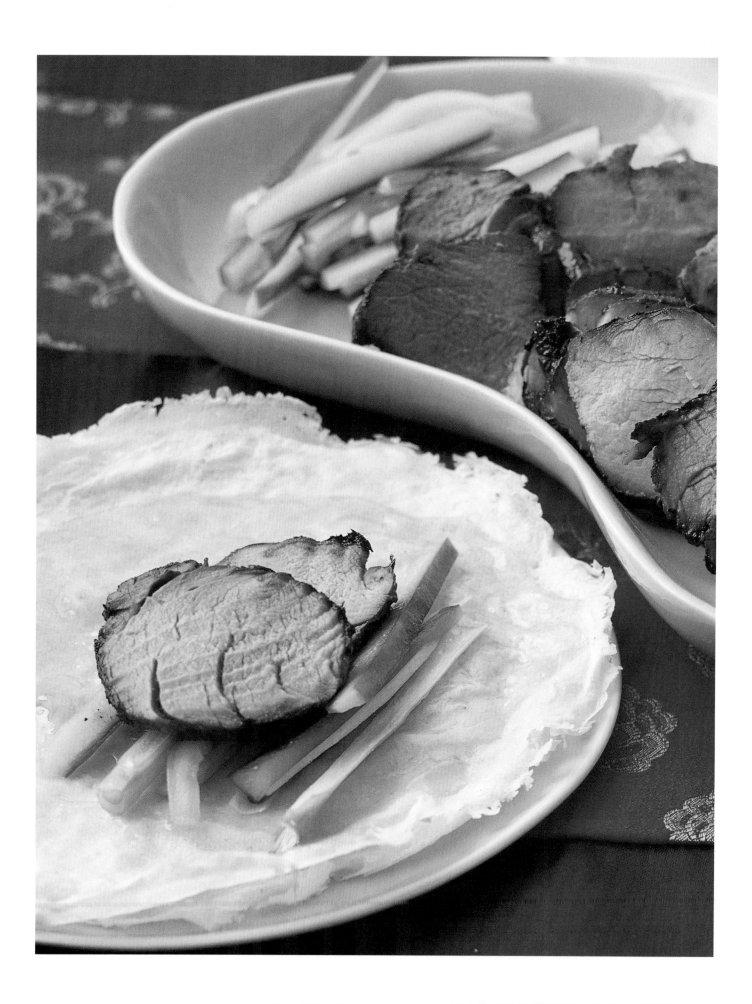

Chinese barbecue pork with pancakes

SERVES 6

sugar	2 tablespoons
light soy sauce	2 tablespoons
hoisin sauce	2 tablespoons
dark soy sauce	2 tablespoons
rice wine	2 tablespoons
yellow bean paste (see Notes)	2 tablespoons
sesame oil	2 teaspoons
five-spice powder	1 teaspoon
garlic cloves	2, crushed
ginger	1 teaspoon finely grated
pork fillet	1 kg (2 lb 4 oz)
honey	1 tablespoon
Peking duck pancakes (see Notes)	24
Lebanese (short) cucumber	1, seeded and cut into 8 cm x 5 mm (3 x ¼ inch) strips
spring onions (scallions)	4 cut into 8 cm x 5 mm (3 x ¼ inch) strips
plum sauce	125 ml (4 fl oz/½ cup)

Put the sugar, light soy sauce, hoisin sauce, dark soy sauce, rice wine, yellow bean paste, sesame oil, five-spice powder, garlic, ginger and ¼ teaspoon ground white pepper in a large, non-metallic bowl. Mix them together well, add the pork fillet and turn it until it is thoroughly coated in the marinade, then cover and refrigerate it for at least 2 hours, or overnight.

Take the pork out of the refrigerator and let it come back to room temperature. Drain the marinade into a small saucepan, add the honey and simmer over low heat for 5 minutes, or until it has reduced slightly.

Preheat the chargrill plate to medium direct heat and cook the pork for 20 minutes, or until it is caramelized and cooked through, turning and basting it with the marinade mixture in the last 5–8 minutes of cooking. Allow the pork fillet to rest for 5 minutes before slicing.

Wrap the pancakes in foil and sit them on a warm place on the grill while the pork is resting so that they heat through without cooking or burning. Put the sliced pork and warm pancakes out with the rest of the fillings and let everyone make their own pancake parcels by wrapping some sliced pork, cucumber, spring onion and plum sauce in a pancake.

Notes Yellow bean paste is made from fermented yellow soy beans and is available from Asian grocery stores. Peking duck pancakes are available frozen from Asian grocery stores or from Chinese barbecue meat shops. Suitable for any barbecue.

Tuna burger with herbed mayonnaise

SERVES 4

garlic cloves	4, crushed
egg yolks	2
light olive oil	250 ml (9 fl oz/1 cup)
flat-leaf (Italian) parsley	3 tablespoons chopped
dill	1 tablespoon chopped
Dijon mustard	2 teaspoons
lemon juice	1 tablespoon
red wine vinegar	1 tablespoon
baby capers in brine	1 tablespoon, drained
anchovy fillets in oil	4, drained
tuna steaks	4 x 150 g (5 oz)
olive oil	2 tablespoons
red onions	2, thinly sliced
bread rolls	4 large round, halved and buttered
mixed lettuce leaves	100 g (4 oz)

Put the garlic and egg yolks in the bowl of a food processor and process them together for 10 seconds. With the motor running, add the oil in a thin, slow stream and when the mixture starts to thicken start adding the oil a little faster. Keep going until all of the oil has been added and the mixture is thick and creamy, then add the parsley, dill, mustard, lemon juice, vinegar, capers and anchovies, and process until smooth. Cover and refrigerate the mayonnaise until you need it.

Preheat the chargrill plate to high direct heat. Brush the tuna steaks with 1 tablespoon of olive oil and cook for 2 minutes on each side, or until they are almost cooked through. Add the remaining oil to the onion, toss to separate and coat the rings, and cook on the flat plate for 2 minutes, or until the onion is soft and caramelized. Toast the bread rolls, buttered side down, on the chargrill plate for 1 minute, or until they are marked and golden.

Put some lettuce, a tuna steak, some of the onion and a dollop of herbed mayonnaise on one half of each roll. Season with salt and pepper, top with the other half of the roll and then serve immediately.

Notes Any left-over mayonnaise will keep for 1 week in an airtight container in the refrigerator. Try tossing it through thickly sliced, steamed potatoes for a delicious snack or side dish. Suitable for a flat or ridged grill plate.

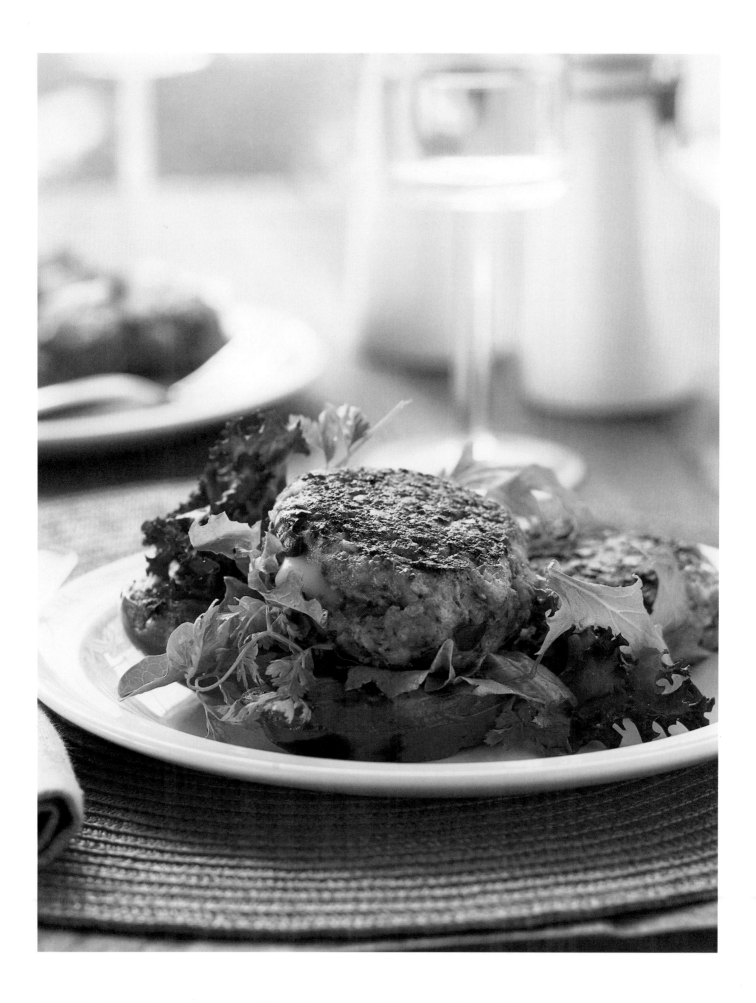

Beef and mozzarella burgers with tomatoes   SERVES 4

minced (ground) beef	500 g (1 lb 2 oz)
fresh breadcrumbs	160 g (5 oz/2 cups)
red onion	1 small, very finely chopped
garlic cloves	4, crushed
basil leaves	3 handfuls, finely shredded
pitted black olives	50 g (2 oz/$^1/_3$ cup), finely chopped
balsamic vinegar	1 tablespoon
egg	1
mozzarella	8 pieces 2 cm x 3 cm x 5 mm ($^3/_4$ x 1$^1/_4$ x $^1/_4$ inch)
olive oil spray	for cooking

chargrilled tomatoes

Roma (plum) tomatoes	6
olive oil	1$^1/_2$ tablespoons

Put the beef, breadcrumbs, red onion, garlic, basil, chopped olives, balsamic vinegar and egg in a large bowl and season well. Use your hands to mix it all together, then cover and refrigerate the mixture for 2 hours.

Divide the beef mixture into eight portions and roll each portion into a ball. Push a piece of mozzarella into the middle of each ball, then push the mince mixture over to cover the hole and flatten the ball to form a patty.

To make the chargrilled tomatoes, slice the tomatoes in half lengthways and toss them with the olive oil. Spray the flat plate with olive oil and preheat it to high direct heat. Cook the tomatoes, cut side down, for 8 minutes then turn them over and cook for another 5 minutes or until they are soft.

Cook the patties on one side for 5 minutes then flip them and cook for another 5 minutes or until completely cooked through and the cheese has melted. Serve the rissoles and chargrilled tomatoes with a fresh green salad.

Note Suitable for a flat or ridged grill plate.

Lamb cutlets with ginger nori butter

SERVES 4

lamb cutlets	16
Japanese plum wine (see Note)	125 ml (4 fl oz/½ cup)
Japanese soy sauce	2 tablespoons
ginger	1 teaspoon finely grated
garlic cloves	2, crushed
sesame oil	few drops
orange sweet potatoes	4 x 200 g (7 oz)
oil	for brushing

ginger nori butter

butter	90 g (3 oz), softened
nori	1½ tablespoons very finely shredded
ginger	2 teaspoons finely grated

Trim the lamb cutlets of any excess fat. Combine the plum wine, soy sauce, grated ginger, garlic and sesame oil, add the cutlets to the marinade and turn them a few times so they are well coated. Cover the dish with plastic wrap and refrigerate it for 3 hours.

To make the ginger nori butter, mash the butter, shredded nori and grated ginger together and season with pepper.

Preheat a covered barbecue to medium indirect heat. Brush the potatoes with a little oil and wrap them in a double layer of foil, put them on the barbecue and replace the lid. Roast the potatoes for 50 minutes, or until they are tender when pierced with a sharp knife, then remove them from the heat and leave the barbecue uncovered.

Drain the marinade into a small saucepan and boil it over high heat for 5 minutes or until it is reduced by about half. Brush the chargrill plate with a little oil and cook the cutlets for 1 minute, then turn them over, brush with the reduced marinade and cook them for another minute. This will give a rare cutlet, so if you like your meat cooked a little more, you'll need to extend the cooking time on each side by a minute or so. Remove the cutlets from the barbecue, brush them with the remaining reduced marinade, cover, and leave them to rest for 3 minutes. Serve the lamb with the orange sweet potatoes topped with nori butter. They are delicious with an Asian leaf salad (try a few handfuls each of mizuna, baby tatsoi and Chinese cabbage) or steamed Asian greens.

Notes Japanese plum wine is available from specialist Japanese grocery stores and from some liquor suppliers. Suitable for a covered barbecue.

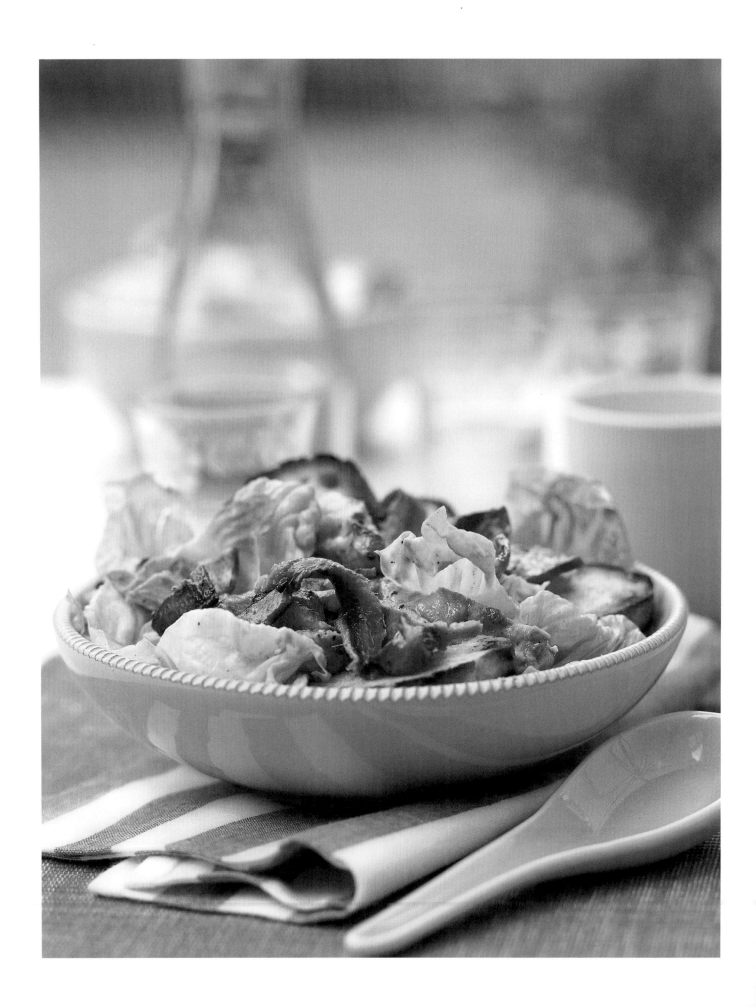

Chicken Caesar salad

SERVES 4–6

Caesar dressing

egg yolk	1
garlic clove	1, crushed
anchovy fillets	3
Dijon mustard	1 teaspoon
oil	125 ml (4 fl oz/½ cup)
lemon juice	1 tablespoon
Worcestershire sauce	½ teaspoon
Parmesan cheese	2 tablespoons grated
boneless, skinless chicken thighs	4, trimmed of fat and sinew
olive oil	80 ml (3 fl oz/⅓ cup)
baguette	12 x 1 cm (½ inch) thick slices
garlic clove	1, halved
bacon	4 rashers
baby cos (romaine) lettuces	2, well washed and drained
anchovies	extra, optional

Put the egg yolk, garlic, anchovy fillets and Dijon mustard in a food processor and blend together. With the motor running, gradually add the oil in a very thin stream and process until the mixture becomes thick. Stir in the lemon juice, Worcestershire sauce and Parmesan, and season with salt and pepper to taste. Put the chicken thighs in a bowl with 1 tablespoon of olive oil, season them well with salt and pepper and turn them so they are coated in the oil.

Preheat the chargrill plate to medium–high direct heat. Brush the baguette slices with the remaining olive oil, and toast them on the chargrill plate for 1 minute on each side, or until they are crisp and marked. Rub both sides of each piece of toast with the cut clove of garlic and keep them warm.

Grill the chicken thighs on the chargrill plate for 5 minutes on each side, or until they are cooked through. Leave the thighs to rest for 1 minute then cut them into 1 cm (½ inch) strips. Cook the bacon for 3 minutes on each side or until it is crispy, then break it into 2 cm (¾ inch) pieces.

Tear the lettuce leaves into bite-sized pieces and toss them in a large bowl with the dressing, bacon and chicken. Serve with the garlic croutons and let people add extra anchovies to taste.

Note Suitable for any type of barbecue.

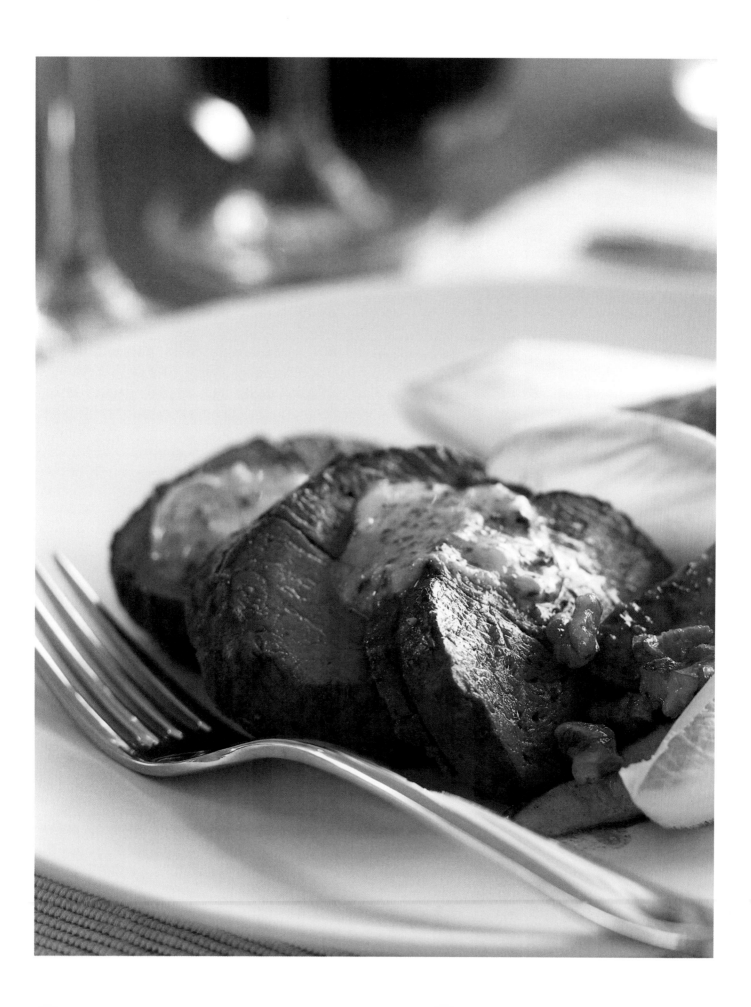

three ways with butter

These butters melt into simple barbecued meat, poultry or seafood and make a straightforward meal that little bit more special. All can be stored, wrapped tightly, in the fridge for up to 1 week, or frozen for 2 to 3 months. Simply slice off the amount you need, as and when you need it. Experiment with different herbs, spices and types of soft cheese to create a range of flavoursome butters that will add versatility to the menu.

BLUE CHEESE BUTTER

Mash together 100 g (4 oz) softened butter, 2 crushed garlic cloves, 100 g (4 oz) Blue Castello cheese and 2 teaspoons finely shredded sage leaves until they are well combined. Form the mixture into a log and wrap it in baking paper, twisting the ends to seal them. Refrigerate the butter until firm, then cut it into 5 mm (1/4 inch) slices and serve at room temperature with barbecued beef. Serves 4.

ROSEMARY MUSTARD BUTTER

Beat 125 g (5 oz) softened butter until light and creamy, add 3 tablespoons wholegrain mustard, 1 tablespoon chopped rosemary and 1 teaspoon each of lemon juice, lemon rind and honey. Mix together until well combined. Spoon the butter down the middle of a piece of plastic wrap, fold up the edges over the butter and roll the mixture into a log shape. Refrigerate until firm. Slice the butter into rounds and serve on top of barbecued lamb or beef. Serves 6.

LEMON AND DILL BUTTER

Beat 90 g (3 oz) softened butter with electric beaters until smooth. Beat in 2 tablespoons finely chopped dill, 1/2 teaspoon finely grated lemon rind and 2 tablespoons lemon juice until well combined. Spoon onto greaseproof paper, shape into a log, roll up and twist the ends to seal. Refrigerate until firm, then cut into thick slices. Serves 6.

blue cheese butter

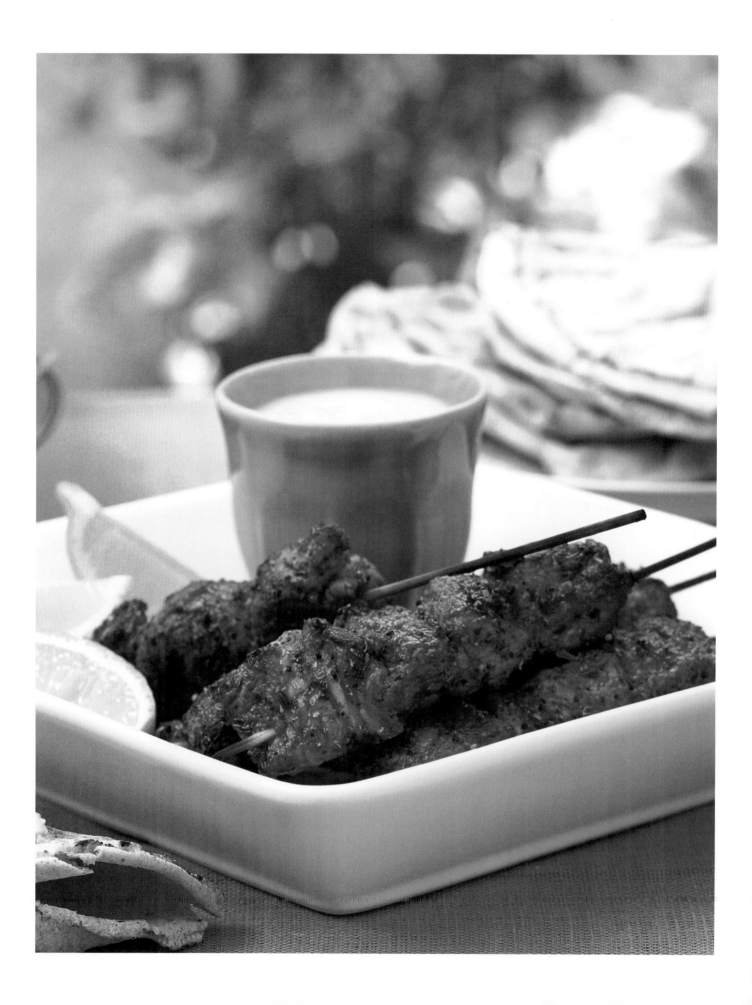

Spice-rubbed pork kebabs with garlic sauce SERVES 4

pork neck fillet	800 g (1 lb 12 oz), trimmed
fennel seeds	2 teaspoons
coriander seeds	2 teaspoons
olive oil	1 tablespoon

garlic sauce

garlic cloves	4, coarsely chopped
white bread	1 thick slice, crusts removed
olive oil	60 ml (2 fl oz/¼ cup)
lemon juice	1½ tablespoons
lemon wedges	to serve
pitta bread	to serve

Soak 8 wooden skewers in cold water for 1 hour and cut the pork into 2 cm (¾ inch) cubes. Dry-fry the fennel and coriander seeds for 30 seconds, or until they are fragrant, then grind them in a spice grinder or mortar and pestle. Mix the ground spices with the olive oil and toss the pork in it until the meat is well coated. Cover the dish and refrigerate it for 2 hours.

To make the garlic sauce, crush the garlic cloves in a mortar and pestle with ½ teaspoon salt until you have a very smooth paste. Tear the bread into pieces and leave it in a bowl with enough warm water to cover it. Let it soak for 5 minutes then squeeze out the bread and add it to the garlic, a little at a time, pounding as you go until you have a smooth paste. Keep pounding as you add the olive oil, 1 tablespoon at a time until it has all been added, then add 3 tablespoons of boiling water, one tablespoon at a time, and stir in the lemon juice. You should end up with a smooth, thick paste.

Thread the pork onto the skewers and season the kebabs well with salt and pepper. Preheat the chargrill plate to medium–high direct heat and grill the kebabs for 10 minutes, or until they are cooked through, turning them halfway through the cooking time. Drizzle the kebabs with a little garlic sauce and put the rest of the sauce in a small bowl to serve at the table. Serve with lemon wedges and warm pitta bread.

Notes You can also use a small food processor to make the garlic sauce. Beware! It has a very strong flavour, so only a little is required. Suitable for any barbecue.

Spicy crab with pepper sauce

SERVES 4–6

blue crabs	2 kg (4 lb 8 oz)
butter	150 g (5 oz)
garlic	2 tablespoons finely chopped
ginger	1 tablespoon finely chopped
red chilli	1 small, seeded and finely chopped
black pepper	3 tablespoons ground
dark soy sauce	2 tablespoons
oyster sauce	2 tablespoons
palm sugar or soft brown sugar	1 tablespoon
spring onion (scallion)	1, green part only, sliced thinly on the diagonal

To prepare the crabs pull back the apron and remove the top shell from each crab (the shell should come off easily and in one piece). Remove the intestine and the grey feathery gills, then use a large sharp knife to cut the crab in half lengthways, leaving the legs attached. Crack the thick part of the legs with the back of a heavy knife or crab crackers to allow the flavours to seep in and to make it easier to extract the meat.

Heat the barbecue flat plate or chargrill plate to medium–high direct heat. Cook the crab pieces for 5–8 minutes on each side, or until they have turned orange and are cooked through. Heat a wok over medium heat (you'll need to do this on the stovetop if you don't have a special wok burner on your barbecue), and stir-fry the butter, garlic, ginger, chilli and pepper together for 30 seconds or until they are fragrant. Add the combined soy and oyster sauces and sugar to the wok, and simmer the sauce for another minute or until it becomes glossy.

Toss the cooked crab in the sauce until completely coated, then arrange it on a serving dish, sprinkle with the spring onion and serve with steamed rice and a green salad. This dish is very rich and very messy to eat — make sure there are plenty of paper towels or napkins on hand to clear up spills.

Note Suitable for any type of barbecue.

Lemon and sage veal chops with rocket

SERVES 4

veal chops	4
olive oil	2 tablespoons
lemon juice	1 tablespoon
lemon zest	4 strips
sage leaves	3 tablespoons roughly chopped
garlic cloves	3, peeled and bruised
lemon wedges	to serve

rocket salad

rocket (arugula)	4 handfuls, washed and picked
avocado	1, sliced
extra virgin olive oil	1½ tablespoons
balsamic vinegar	2 teaspoons

Trim any fat and sinew from the chops and put them in a shallow, non-metallic dish with the olive oil, lemon juice, lemon zest, sage and garlic. Turn the chops so that they are evenly coated, then season them with freshly ground black pepper, cover and refrigerate for 4 hours or overnight.

Put the rocket in a large serving bowl and scatter the avocado over it. Drizzle the olive oil and balsamic vinegar over the salad, season it with salt and black pepper and toss gently.

Preheat the chargrill plate to medium–high direct heat. Remove the chops from the marinade, season with salt and chargrill them for 5–6 minutes on each side, or until they are cooked to your liking. Remove the chops from the barbecue, cover them loosely with foil and let them rest for 5 minutes.

Put the chops on a serving dish, drizzle them with any juices that have been released while they rested and serve with the rocket salad and lemon wedges.

Note Suitable for any barbecue.

Spiced duck with peach and chilli salad

SERVES 4

peaches	6 ripe
lime	1, plus 1 tablespoon lime juice, extra
extra virgin olive oil	1 tablespoon
red chilli	1 small, seeded and thinly sliced
mint leaves	2 tablespoons chopped
duck breasts	4
ground coriander	2 teaspoons
lime wedges	

Dip the peaches into a saucepan of boiling water for 5 seconds, then plunge them into iced water. Remove the skins, which should slip off easily. Cut each peach in half, remove the stone, then cut each half into eight wedges. Peel the lime, removing all the pith, and separate the lime sections by carefully cutting each piece away from the membrane. Toss the peach slices with the lime segments, extra lime juice, olive oil, chilli and mint, and season with a little pepper.

Trim the duck breasts of fat and sinew, and sprinkle each breast with the ground coriander.

Preheat the flat plate to medium direct heat and cook the duck on the flat plate for 4 minutes or until the skin is golden, then turn it and cook for another 4 minutes. Turn breasts over again and cook them for 1 minute longer to make the skin crispy, then leave to rest in a warm place for 10 minutes.

Slice each breast into four pieces on the diagonal and serve them with the peach salad and lime wedges.

Note Suitable for a flat or ridged grill plate.

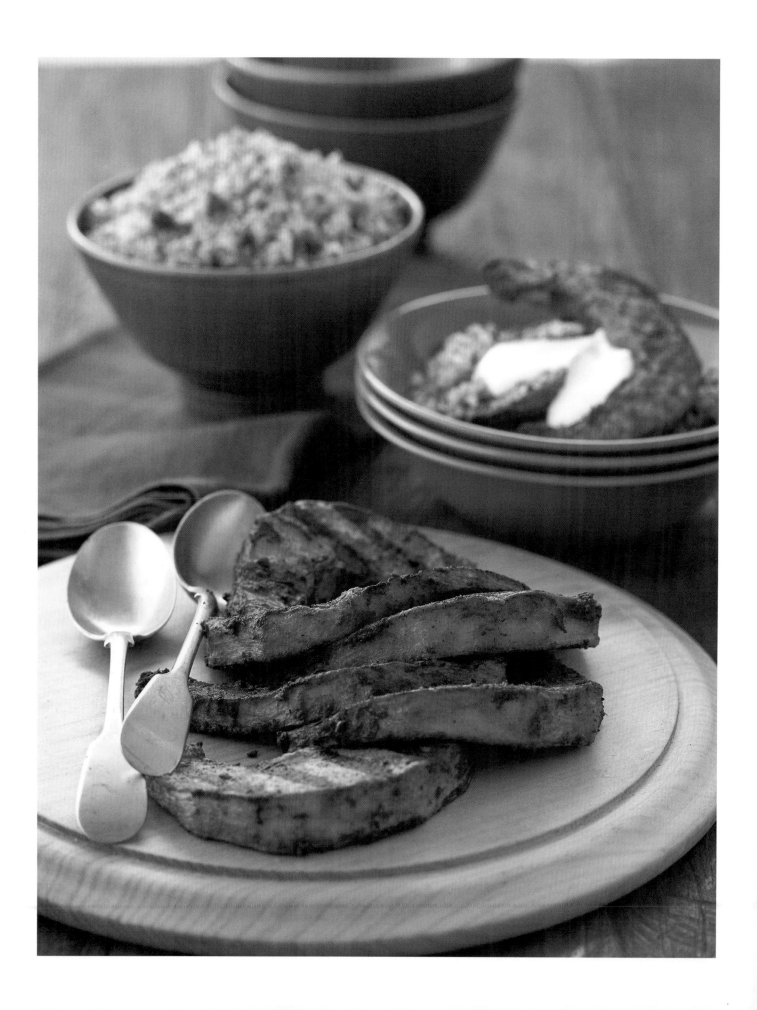

Moroccan pumpkin on pistachio couscous SERVES 4–6

vegetable stock	250 ml (9 fl oz/1 cup)
instant couscous	185 g (7 oz/1 cup)
butter	1 tablespoon
garlic cloves	2, crushed
onion	1 small, finely diced
flat-leaf (Italian) parsley	2 tablespoons finely chopped
coriander (cilantro) leaves	2 tablespoons finely chopped
pistachio nuts	35 g (1 oz/¼ cup) roasted, shelled and roughly chopped
ras el hanout or Moroccan spice blend (see Notes)	2 tablespoons
Greek-style plain yoghurt	250 g (9 oz/1 cup)
lemon juice	1 tablespoon
honey	1 tablespoon
pumpkin	1 kg (2 lb 4 oz)
olive oil	2 tablespoons

Bring the stock to the boil, pour it over the couscous and stir to combine them. Cover the bowl with plastic wrap and leave it for 10 minutes, or until all of the stock has been absorbed.

Melt the butter in a small frying pan, add the garlic and onion and cook them over low heat for 5 minutes, or until they are softened. Add the onion mixture to the couscous with the parsley, coriander, pistachio nuts and 2 teaspoons of the spice mix, stir it together and season to taste. Cover the bowl with plastic wrap and keep it warm.

Put the yoghurt in a small bowl, stir in the lemon juice and honey, and season to taste.

Peel the pumpkin, cut it into 2 cm (¾ inch) thick pieces and toss it in a bowl with the oil and the remaining spice mix. Preheat a covered or kettle barbecue to medium direct heat. Grill the pumpkin, covered, for 45 minutes, or until it is golden all over and cooked through. Pile the couscous onto a serving plate, top it with the grilled pumpkin pieces and serve with the yoghurt dressing.

Notes Ras el hanout is a Moroccan spice mix, and is available from gourmet food stores. The taste of this dish will rely on the quality of the spices used, so if you have time, make your own. Dry-fry 6 cardamom pods, ½ teaspoon black pepper and 1 teaspoon fennel seeds until fragrant. Allow the spices to cool, then grind in a spice grinder or mortar and pestle and mix with ½ teaspoon ground cinnamon, 1 teaspoon turmeric, ½ teaspoon cayenne pepper, 2 teaspoons mild paprika, 1 teaspoon ground cumin, ½ teaspoon allspice and 1 teaspoon salt. The spice mix can be stored in an airtight container for up to 2 months. Suitable for a covered barbecue.

Snapper envelope with ginger

dressing	
spring onion (scallion)	1
coriander (cilantro) leaves	1 small handful
ginger	1 teaspoon finely grated
lime juice	2 tablespoons
fish sauce	1 tablespoon
sesame oil	½ teaspoon
whole snapper	1 (about 1.8–2 kg/4 lb–4 lb 8 oz)
sea salt	to season
lime	1
spring onions (scallions)	4
coriander (cilantro) leaves	2 large handfuls
ginger	1 tablespoon finely grated
canola oil spray	for cooking

To make the dressing, finely slice the green part of the spring onion and the coriander leaves, and mix them together with the ginger, lime juice, fish sauce and sesame oil.

Check that the fish has been thoroughly scaled, then wash it under cold running water and dry with paper towels. In the thickest part of the flesh make diagonal cuts 1.5 cm (⅝ inch) apart in one direction, then in the other direction, so that the flesh is scored in a diamond pattern. Lightly season the fish with sea salt and freshly ground black pepper.

Peel the lime, removing all the pith, with a small, sharp knife and separate the lime sections by carefully cutting each piece away from the membrane. Slice the spring onions on the diagonal, mix them with the coriander leaves, lime segments and ginger, and stuff the mixture into the cavity of the fish.

Lightly spray a double layer of foil with canola oil, making sure it is large enough to wrap around the fish and totally enclose it. Fold the foil around the fish and seal the edges tightly.

Preheat a kettle or covered barbecue to medium indirect heat. Put the fish in the middle of the barbecue and cook it, covered, for 10 minutes. Use a large metal spatula to turn the fish and cook it for another 8–10 minutes, or until it flakes when tested in the thickest part of the flesh.

When the fish is cooked, open the foil and slide it onto a plate. Pour the cooking juices over the fish, drizzle the dressing over the top and serve straight away. It is delicious with steamed jasmine rice and a green salad.

Note Suitable for a covered barbecue.

Lamb burger

ground cumin	1 tablespoon
Greek-style plain yoghurt	250 g (9 oz/1 cup)
Lebanese (short) cucumber	½, grated
mint leaves	1 tablespoon finely chopped
olive oil	2 tablespoons
onion	1, finely chopped
garlic cloves	2, crushed
minced (ground) lamb	800 g (1 lb 12 oz)
flat-leaf (Italian) parsley	2 tablespoons finely chopped
coriander (cilantro) leaves	2 tablespoons finely chopped
red capsicums (peppers)	2, quartered and seeded
red onions	2, thinly sliced
olive oil spray	for cooking
Turkish bread	1 loaf, cut into 4 pieces and split horizontally
baby rocket (arugula) leaves	4 handfuls

Dry-fry 1 teaspoon ground cumin in a pan over medium heat for 30 seconds, or until fragrant. Put the yoghurt, cucumber, mint and dry-fried cumin in a small bowl and mix it together. Cover the bowl and refrigerate it until needed.

Heat half the oil in a frying pan and cook the onion over medium heat for 2–3 minutes or until it is softened. Add the garlic and remaining cumin, cook it for another minute, then allow the mixture to cool.

Put the onion mixture in a large bowl with the mince, parsley and coriander, season with salt and pepper and mix it together with your hands. Divide the mixture into four portions, and shape each portion into a 2 cm (¾ inch) thick patty.

Heat the barbecue to medium–high direct heat. Toss the capsicum with the remaining oil and cook it on the flat plate for 6 minutes on each side or until it is softened and lightly charred. Grill the lamb patties on the flat plate for 5–6 minutes each side or until they are done.

Spray the red onion with the olive oil spray and cook it on the flat plate for 2–3 minutes or until it is soft and golden. Toast the bread, cut side down, on the chargrill plate for 1–2 minutes or until it is marked and golden.

To assemble the burgers, put some rocket on four of the bread slices. Put a pattie on top, then the capsicum and onion. Dollop 2–3 tablespoons of the yoghurt mixture on each and season with salt and freshly ground black pepper, then top with the remaining bread slices and serve them straight away.

Note Suitable for a flat or ridged grill plate.

Beef with blue cheese butter

beef eye fillet (thick end)	1 kg (2 lb 4 oz), trimmed
olive oil	1 tablespoon
blue cheese butter (page 73)	1 quantity

pear and walnut salad

walnut oil	60 ml (2 fl oz/¼ cup)
sherry vinegar	1¼ tablespoons
Dijon mustard	1 teaspoon
pears	3 ripe, halved, cored, cut into 1 cm (½ inch) thick wedges
butter	50 g (2 oz), melted
soft brown sugar	1 tablespoon
witlof (chicory/Belgian endive)	2 heads, leaves separated
walnut pieces	85 g (3 oz/⅔ cup), toasted and chopped

To make the dressing, whisk the walnut oil, vinegar, mustard and some freshly ground black pepper in a bowl. Put the pears, melted butter and sugar in a bowl and toss them together until the pears are well coated in the butter.

Cut the beef into four thick, equal pieces and tie a piece of string around the edge of each so it will keep its shape during cooking. Brush both sides of the steaks with the oil and season them with freshly ground black pepper. Heat the barbecue to medium–high direct heat and cook the beef on the chargrill plate for 6–7 minutes on each side for medium, or to your liking. Cook the pear slices on the flat plate for 1 minute each side or until they are golden and slightly caramelized, basting with the butter and sugar mixture during cooking.

Put two slices of blue cheese butter on top of each steak as soon as you remove it from the barbecue and remove the string. Put the witlof in a large bowl, add the dressing, walnuts and pears and toss well, then serve the salad with the beef medallions.

Notes Any leftover butter can be wrapped in baking paper and foil, and frozen for up to 2 months for later use. It is also delicious with chicken and pork. Suitable for a flat or ridged grill plate.

three ways with dips

Barbecues (and, in fact, any form of casual entertaining for a crowd) aren't complete without a few dips — something to nibble on with a drink in hand while the barbecue gets under way and to stave off those hunger pangs until the main dishes are ready. Serve these light and flavoursome dips with a variety of breads and crackers. Flatbreads very briefly heated on the barbecue grill and torn into pieces are particularly good for scooping up dips.

hummus

Soak 220 g (8 oz/1 cup) dried chickpeas in 1 litre (4 cups) of water overnight. Drain and place in a large saucepan with 2 litres (8 cups) water, or enough to cover the chickpeas by 5 cm (2 inches). Bring to the boil, then reduce the heat and simmer for $1^1/4$ hours, or until the chickpeas are very tender. Skim any froth from the surface. Drain well, reserve the cooking liquid and leave until cool enough to handle. Pick over for any loose skins and discard. Transfer the chickpeas to a food processor. Add 2 tablespoons tahini, 4 crushed garlic cloves, 2 teaspoons ground cumin, 80 ml (3 fl oz/$^1/_3$ cup) lemon juice, 60 ml (2 fl oz/$^1/_4$ cup) olive oil, a large pinch of cayenne pepper and $1^1/2$ teaspoons salt and process until thick and smooth. With the motor running, gradually add 185 ml (6 fl oz/$^3/_4$ cup) of the reserved cooking liquid to form a smooth, creamy purée. Season with salt or extra lemon juice. Spread onto a flat bowl or plate, drizzle with oil, sprinkle with a pinch of paprika and scatter a little parsley on top. Serve with pitta or pide breads that have been warmed on the barbecue.

guacamole

Mash 2 ripe avocados with $2^1/2$ tablespoons lime juice, 3 finely sliced spring onions (scallions), 1 large handful coriander (cilantro) leaves and 1 teaspoon finely chopped chilli, and season the mixture to taste. Cover the guacamole with plastic wrap, resting the plastic directly on the surface of the mixture, and refrigerate until you are ready to use it. Serve with pitta or pide breads that have been warmed on the barbecue.

tzatziki

Cut 2 Lebanese (short) cucumbers in half lengthways, scoop out the seeds and discard. Leaving the skin on, coarsley grate the cucumber into a small colander. Sprinkle with salt and leave over a bowl for 15 minutes to drain off any bitter juices. Meanwhile, stir together 400 g (13 oz/$1^2/_3$ cups) Greek-style plain yoghurt, 4 crushed garlic cloves, 3 tablespoons finely chopped mint and 1 tablespoon lemon juice. Rinse the cucumber under cold water and then, taking small handfuls, squeeze out any extra moisture. Combine the grated cucumber with the yoghurt mixture and season well. Serve with pitta or pide bread or as a sauce with barbecued chicken.

Hummus

Honey-roasted pork fillet with carrots

SERVES 6–8

ginger	1 tablespoon finely grated
garlic cloves	6
soy sauce	80 ml (3 fl oz/1/3 cup)
oil	2 tablespoons
pork neck or blade roast	2 kg (4 lb 8 oz) piece
honey	2 tablespoons

parsley carrots

baby carrots	600 g (1 lb 5 oz)
olive oil	2 teaspoons
butter	30 g (1 oz)
flat-leaf (Italian) parsley	2 tablespoons finely chopped

Mix the ginger, garlic, soy sauce and oil in a large, non-metallic bowl. Put the pork in the marinade and turn it so that it is well coated, then cover the bowl and refrigerate it overnight.

Bring a saucepan of salted water to the boil, and blanch the carrots for 3 minutes or until they start to soften. Drain and refresh them under cold water and pat them dry with paper towels. Just before the pork is due to be ready, toss the carrots in olive oil and season them with salt and pepper.

Remove the pork from the marinade, pour the marinade into a small saucepan and simmer it over low heat for 5 minutes or until it is slightly reduced. Stir the honey into the warm marinade and remove it from the heat. Preheat a kettle or covered barbecue to low–medium indirect heat, then put the pork in the middle of the barbecue and roast it, covered, for 45 minutes or until it is cooked through. In the last 10 minutes of cooking, baste the roast all over with the reduced marinade. Be careful not to let any of the marinade splash onto the grill, as it may burn and stick. Remove the roast from the barbecue and put it on a tray, covered, to rest for 10 minutes.

While the roast is resting, cook the carrots on the chargrill plate for 5 minutes, or until they are charred and golden all over, then toss the carrots with the butter and parsley until they are well coated. Season to taste with salt and freshly ground black pepper.

Carve the roast and serve it with any pan juices left in the tray and the warm parsley carrots.

Note Suitable for a covered barbecue.

Types of barbecue

There are two main methods of cooking on a barbecue. The first is to cook food over direct heat, for example over a wood fire or barbecue fuel briquettes located directly under a grill or plate. The food must be turned during cooking so that it cooks evenly on both sides. The other method is to use indirect heat, for which you will need a barbecue with some kind of hood or cover. This method of cooking works a bit like an oven, by circulating the heat around the food, and it is mainly used for roasting larger cuts of meat, giving them a distinctive barbecue flavour.

wood-burning fixed barbecues

These are the traditional, backyard barbecue — usually a fairly simple construction in the form of an elevated grill plate with a fire burning underneath. Although easy to use and available to anyone with some clear space, a few bricks and a grill, the basic design lends itself only to fairly simple methods of cooking. Heat regulation is usually achieved by adjusting the fire and waiting for it to reach the right temperature, although it's more desirable to let the flames die down and cook over a pile of glowing embers which give off a more constant heat.

kettle barbecues

These are portable, come in a range of sizes and are designed for both direct and indirect cooking. A kettle barbecue has a rounded base which holds barbecue fuel briquettes on a metal grill. If you want to cook with direct heat, simply grill the food over the coals. If you want to cook using the indirect method, arrange the briquettes in two piles on opposite sides of the bottom grill and put a drip-tray between them before inserting the top grill. To give the heat a boost, open the vents in the outer shell of the barbecue — this will allow air to circulate, making the briquettes burn faster and hotter. To keep the temperature a little cooler, leave the vents closed.

gas barbecues

These are available in a huge variety of sizes and shapes, from small portables to huge, wagon-style barbecues that come with a hood, rotisserie and workbench on the side. They are convenient and simple to operate, usually requiring only 10 minutes or so to heat up, and the turn of a knob to regulate temperature. Some work by means of a flame under the barbecue plate, while others use the flame to heat a bed of reusable volcanic rock. If your barbecue has a lid or hood, you can also cook using indirect heat.

electric barbecues

These operate on a principle similar to that of gas barbecues, by heating the grill plate on which the food is cooked. They can be less convenient than a gas barbecue as they require access to an electricity outlet and the heat produced may not be as even or as strong as that produced by a gas or solid-fuel barbecue.

Teriyaki baby octopus

SERVES 4

sake	125 ml (4 fl oz/½ cup)
mirin	125 ml (4 fl oz/½ cup)
dark soy sauce	125 ml (4 fl oz/½ cup)
caster (superfine) sugar	1 tablespoon
ginger	2 teaspoons grated
garlic cloves	2, finely chopped
baby octopus	1 kg (2 lb 4 oz)

asian salad

nori	2 sheets, cut into 3 cm x 5 mm (1¼ x ¼ inch) pieces
rice wine vinegar	2 tablespoons seasoned
lemon juice	2 teaspoons
sesame oil	¼ teaspoon
canola oil	2 teaspoons
mizuna leaves	60 g (2 oz)
snow pea shoots	60 g (2 oz)
Lebanese (short) cucumbers	2, shaved
daikon	½, shaved

Combine the sake, mirin, dark soy sauce and sugar in a small saucepan. Bring mixture to the boil over medium heat and boil, stirring until all sugar has dissolved, then add ginger and garlic and remove saucepan from the heat. Leave the mixture to cool for 30 minutes.

Meanwhile, to prepare octopus, use a small knife to carefully cut between head and tentacles of octopus, just below eyes. Push beak out and up through the tentacles with your finger, then remove eyes from head of octopus by cutting off a small disc and discarding it. To clean octopus tube, carefully slit through one side, avoiding the ink sac, and scrape out any gut. Rinse inside under running water to remove any remaining gut and cut it in half. Wash rest of octopus thoroughly under running water, pulling skin away from the tube and tentacles. If the octopus are large, cut the tentacles into quarters.

Put octopus in a large, non-metallic bowl. Whisk the teriyaki marinade, making sure that it is well combined, then pour it over the octopus, stirring so that the octopus is thoroughly coated. Cover and marinate it in the refrigerator for at least 2 hours, or overnight.

Preheat chargrill plate to medium direct heat. Remove octopus from the teriyaki marinade and cook them for 2–3 minutes, or until they are cooked through, curled and glazed. To make the salad, toast nori on a preheated barbecue plate for 5 minutes to make it crispy. Make the dressing by whisking together the rice wine vinegar, lemon juice, sesame oil and canola oil. Toss mizuna, snow pea shoots, cucumber, daikon and nori with the dressing. Arrange the octopus on top of the salad to serve.

Note Suitable for a flat or ridged grill plate.

Lebanese chicken with eggplant salad

Greek-style plain yoghurt	250 g (9 oz/1 cup)
soft brown sugar	2 teaspoons
garlic cloves	4, crushed
ground cumin	3 teaspoons
ground coriander	1½ teaspoons
flat-leaf (Italian) parsley	3 tablespoons chopped
lemon juice	60 ml (2 fl oz/¼ cup)
chicken	1 x 1.8 kg (4 lb), cut into 10 serving pieces
olive oil spray	for cooking

eggplant, tomato and sumac salad

eggplants (aubergines)	2, cut into 1 cm (½ inch) thick rounds
olive oil	100 ml (3 fl oz)
tomatoes	5 large ripe
red onion	1 small, finely sliced
mint leaves	4 tablespoons roughly chopped
flat-leaf (Italian) parsley	4 tablespoons roughly chopped
sumac (see Notes)	2 teaspoons
lemon juice	2 tablespoons

Put the yoghurt, brown sugar, garlic, cumin, coriander, parsley and lemon juice in a large, non-metallic bowl and mix together. Add the chicken pieces to the marinade and turn them so that they are completely coated, then cover and refrigerate for at least 2 hours, or overnight.

To make the salad, put the eggplant slices in a colander, and sprinkle them with salt. Leave the eggplant for 30 minutes to allow some of the bitter juices to drain away, then rinse the slices and pat them dry with paper towels. Brush both sides of each slice with 2 tablespoons of the olive oil, then chargrill them for 5 minutes on each side or until they are cooked through. Let the slices cool slightly and cut them in half.

Cut the tomatoes into wedges and arrange in a serving bowl with the eggplant and onion. Scatter the mint, parsley and sumac over the top, then put the lemon juice and remaining olive oil in a small, screw-top jar, season, and shake it up. Drizzle the dressing over the salad and toss it gently.

Lightly spray the barbecue plates with oil, then preheat the barbecue to medium direct heat. Take the chicken pieces out of the marinade and season them with salt and pepper. Cook the chicken pieces on the flat plate, turning them frequently, for 20–30 minutes, or until they are cooked through. If you have a barbecue with a lid, cover the barbecue while the chicken is cooking. This way, the breast pieces will take only 15 minutes to cook, while the pieces on the bone will take about 10 minutes longer. Serve the chicken with the eggplant, tomato and sumac salad.

Notes Sumac is a spice made from crushing the dried sumac berry. It has a mild lemony flavour and is used extensively in many cuisines, from North Africa and the Middle East, to India and Asia. Suitable for any barbecue.

Marinated vegetable salad

SERVES 4

capsicums (peppers)	2 large red, cored and seeded
eggplants (aubergines)	5 slender, cut into 1 cm (½ inch) slices on the diagonal
asparagus spears	300 g (11 oz), trimmed and halved
zucchini (courgettes)	4, cut into 1 cm (½ inch) slices on the diagonal
field mushrooms	300 g (11 oz) small, quartered
olive oil	125 ml (4 fl oz/½ cup)
garlic cloves	4, crushed
bocconcini	200 g (7 oz), sliced
baby rocket (arugula) leaves	150 g (5 oz)
balsamic vinegar	1 tablespoon

pesto

basil leaves	2 large handfuls
pine nuts	50 g (2 oz/⅓ cup), toasted
garlic cloves	3, crushed
sea salt	½ teaspoon
olive oil	125 ml (4 fl oz/½ cup)
Parmesan cheese	20 g (1 oz/¼ cup) finely grated
pecorino cheese	20 g (1 oz/¼ cup) finely grated

Cut the capsicums into quarters, then each quarter into three strips. Put the capsicum, eggplant, asparagus, zucchini and mushrooms in a large bowl, pour in the combined oil and garlic, season with salt and freshly ground pepper, and toss it all together. Leave the vegetables to marinate for 1 hour, tossing occasionally.

To make the pesto, put the basil, pine nuts, garlic, salt and oil in a food processor and process until it is smooth. Stir in the Parmesan and pecorino, then cover the bowl until you are ready to use it.

Heat the flat plate to high and cook the vegetables, turning, for 7–8 minutes, or until they are soft and golden. Arrange the grilled vegetables on a serving plate with the bocconcini, and toss the rocket with the vinegar. Drizzle the vegetables with the pesto and serve them immediately with warmed, crusty bread rolls.

Note Suitable for a flat or ridged grill plate.

Thai beef salad

lime juice	80 ml (3 fl oz/⅓ cup)
fish sauce	2 tablespoons
palm sugar or soft brown sugar	2 teaspoons grated
garlic clove	1, crushed
coriander (cilantro) roots and stems	1 tablespoon finely chopped
lemon grass	1 stem, white part only, finely chopped
red chillies	2 small, finely sliced
beef eye fillet steaks	2 x 200 g (7 oz)
mixed salad leaves	150 g (5 oz)
red onion	½, cut into thin wedges
coriander (cilantro) leaves	1 large handful
mint leaves	1 handful, torn
cherry tomatoes	250 g (9 oz), halved
Lebanese (short) cucumber	1, halved lengthways and thinly sliced on the diagonal

Combine the lime juice, fish sauce, palm sugar, garlic, chopped coriander, lemon grass and chilli until the sugar has dissolved.

Preheat the chargrill plate to medium–high direct heat and cook the steaks for 4 minutes on each side, or until medium. Let the steaks cool, then slice them thinly across the grain.

Put the salad leaves, onion, coriander leaves, mint, tomatoes and cucumber in a large bowl, add the beef and dressing, toss them together and serve immediately.

Note Suitable for any type of barbecue.

Sage and ricotta-stuffed chicken

fresh ricotta cheese	250 g (9 oz/1 cup), well drained
sage leaves	1 tablespoon, shredded
garlic cloves	2, crushed
lemon zest	1½ teaspoons
Parmesan cheese	40 g (1½ oz/⅓ cup) finely grated
boneless, skinless chicken breast fillets	4, tenderloins removed
prosciutto	8 thin slices
olive oil	for brushing

baby spinach salad

baby spinach leaves	150 g (5 oz)
small black olives	100 g (4 oz/½ cup)
olive oil	2 tablespoons
lemon juice	1 tablespoon
sea salt	

Combine the ricotta, sage, garlic, zest and Parmesan until they are well combined. Use a sharp knife to cut a large pocket into the side of each chicken breast and fill each pocket with a quarter of the ricotta mixture. Pin the pockets closed with toothpicks and wrap each breast in two slices of prosciutto, securing it with a toothpick.

To make the spinach salad, toss the spinach in a large serving bowl with the olives and the combined olive oil and lemon juice. Season with sea salt and freshly ground black pepper.

Heat the flat plate to medium direct heat, brush the chicken parcels with olive oil and season them with freshly ground black pepper. Cook them for 8 minutes on each side, or until they are cooked through. Serve the chicken with the salad.

Note Suitable for a flat or ridged grill plate.

Pork and fennel sausages with onion relish   MAKES 8

minced (ground) pork	750 g (1 lb 1o oz)
fresh breadcrumbs	40 g (1½ oz/½ cup)
garlic cloves	2, crushed
fennel seeds	3 teaspoons, coarsely crushed
orange zest	1 teaspoon finely grated
thyme leaves	2 teaspoons chopped
flat-leaf (Italian) parsley	1 handful, chopped
oil	for brushing
baguette	1 long, cut into 4 pieces, or 4 long crusty rolls
butter	50 g (2 oz), softened
rocket (arugula) leaves	60 g (2 oz)
extra virgin olive oil	1 tablespoon
balsamic vinegar	1 teaspoon

onion relish

butter	50 g (2 oz)
red onions	2, thinly sliced
soft brown sugar	1 tablespoon
balsamic vinegar	2 tablespoons

Put the mince, breadcrumbs, garlic, fennel seeds, zest, thyme and parsley in a large bowl, season well with salt and freshly ground black pepper and mix it all together with your hands. Cover the mixture and refrigerate it for 4 hours or overnight.

To make the onion relish, melt the butter in a heavy-based saucepan, add the onion and cook, stirring occasionally, over low heat for 1o minutes, or until the onion is softened, but not browned. Add the brown sugar and vinegar, and continue to cook it for another 30 minutes, stirring regularly.

Preheat the flat plate to medium direct heat. Divide the pork mixture into eight portions and use wet hands to mould each portion into a flattish sausage shape. Lightly brush the sausages with oil and cook them for 8 minutes on each side, or until they are cooked through.

To assemble, split the rolls down the middle and butter them. Toss the rocket leaves with the olive oil and balsamic vinegar, and put some of the leaves in each of the rolls. Top with a sausage and some of the onion relish.

Note Suitable for a flat or ridged grill plate.

Lamb stuffed with olives, feta and oregano   SERVES 4

pitted Kalamata olives	85 g (3 oz/½ cup)
garlic cloves	3, crushed
olive oil	100 ml (3 fl oz)
lamb sirloin (see Notes)	800 g (1 lb 12 oz), trimmed
feta cheese	90 g (3 oz), crumbled
oregano leaves	2 tablespoons, finely shredded
lemon juice	80 ml (3 fl oz/⅓ cup)

Put the Kalamata olives in a food processor or blender with the garlic and 2 tablespoons of olive oil, and blend until it is smooth. Season to taste with freshly ground black pepper.

Prepare the sirloin by cutting horizontally most of the way through the piece, starting at one end, leaving a small join at the other end. Open out the lamb so you have a piece half as thick and twice as long as you started with.

Spread the olive and garlic paste in a thin, even layer over the cut surface of the lamb, then crumble the feta over the top and scatter with the chopped oregano. Roll the lamb tightly, starting with one of the long cut edges, and then tie the whole length with cooking twine, so that the olive filling is contained and secure.

Put the lamb into a dish large enough to hold it lying flat and drizzle it with the lemon juice and remaining olive oil, turning to make sure that all of the lamb is well coated. Cover the dish and refrigerate it for 3 hours.

Prepare a chargrill plate to medium–high direct heat. Season the lamb and grill it, turning to brown each side, for 10 minutes, or until cooked to your liking. Remove from the barbecue and let it rest, covered, for 5 minutes. Use a very sharp knife to cut the roll into 5 cm (2 inch) pieces on the diagonal and serve it immediately with a mixed green salad.

Notes Use the thick end of the sirloin for this recipe. Suitable for any barbecue.

Smoked trout with lemon and dill butter

lemon and dill butter

butter	125 g (5 oz) softened
lemon juice	2 tablespoons
dill	2 tablespoons finely chopped
lemon zest	½ teaspoon
small garlic clove	1, crushed
hickory woodchips	6
rainbow trout	4
oil	for brushing

Mash together the butter, lemon juice, dill, zest and garlic, shape it into a log and wrap it in greaseproof paper, twisting the ends to seal them. Refrigerate the butter until it is firm, then cut it into 1 cm (½ inch) slices and leave it at room temperature until ready to use it.

Preheat a kettle barbecue to low indirect heat, allow the coals to burn down to ash, then add three of the hickory woodchips to each side.

Brush the skin of the fish with oil. When the woodchips begin to smoke, put the trout on the barbecue, replace the cover and smoke them for 15 minutes or until they are cooked through. Remove the fish from the grill, gently peel off the skin and top them with the lemon and dill butter while they are still hot. Smoked trout are delicious with boiled new potatoes and a green salad, and can also be served cold.

Notes Like barbecuing, smoking is a simple process with a delicious result. Special woodchips are commercially available which will give off a wonderfully scented smoke and infuse your food with a distinctive flavour. Never use wood that is not specifically intended for smoking food, as many woods are chemically treated and may make the food poisonous. To smoke food, soak six woodchips in water for 1 hour and prepare a kettle barbecue for indirect cooking. When the briquettes are ready, add three woodchips to each side and close the lid until the chips begin to smoke, then cook the food according to the recipe, lifting the lid as little as possible so you don't lose too much of the smoke. Smoking does not work in a gas or electric barbecue as the chips need to burn to infuse their aromatic flavour.

the perfect satay chicken

Cut 500 g (1 lb 2 oz) boneless, skinless chicken thighs into 1 cm (½ inch) wide strips and put in a bowl. Add 1 crushed garlic clove, 2 teaspoons finely grated ginger and 3 teaspoons fish sauce and turn the chicken so that it is well coated. Cover the bowl and leave it in the refrigerator for 1 hour. Soak 12 wooden skewers in cold water for 1 hour.

To make the satay sauce, heat 2 teaspoons peanut oil in a saucepan over medium heat, then add 4 finely chopped Asian shallots, 4 crushed garlic cloves, 2 teaspoons finely chopped ginger and 2 small seeded and finely chopped chillies. Stir the mixture constantly with a wooden spoon for 5 minutes, or until the shallots are golden. Reduce the heat to low, add 125 g (5 oz/½ cup) peanut butter, 185 ml (6 fl oz/¾ cup) coconut milk, 2 teaspoons soy sauce, 2 teaspoons grated palm sugar (or soft brown sugar), 1½ tablespoons fish sauce, 1 kaffir lime leaf and 1½ tablespoons lime juice and simmer for 10 minutes, or until thickened. Remove the lime leaf and keep the sauce warm while you cook the chicken.

Preheat the chargrill plate to medium–high direct heat. Thread two or three chicken strips onto each skewer, without crowding them, and grill the chicken for 10 minutes, or until it is cooked through, turning after 5 minutes. Serve with the sauce. Serves 4.

Chicken salad with rocket and cannellini beans

SERVES 4

lemon juice	1/3 cup (80 ml/2¾ fl oz)
garlic	3 cloves, crushed
brown sugar	1 teaspoon soft
basil	¼ cup (15 g/½ oz) fresh, finely chopped
olive oil	½ cup (125 ml/4 fl oz)
chicken breast	4 fillets
cannellini beans	400 g (13 oz) can, rinsed and drained
rocket leaves	100 g (3½ oz) small

Whisk together the lemon juice, garlic, sugar, basil and olive oil.

Pour a third of the dressing over the chicken to coat. Cook the chicken on a hot, lightly oiled barbecue grill or flatplate for 4 minutes on each side, or until cooked through.

Meanwhile, combine the beans and rocket with the remaining dressing, toss well and season. Slice the chicken and serve over the rocket and beans.

Hoisin lamb with and Asian rice salad

SERVES 4

lamb loin	800 g (1 lb 12 oz)
hoisin sauce	60 ml (2 fl oz/¼ cup)
soy sauce	2 tablespoons
garlic cloves	2, bruised
ginger	1 tablespoon grated
olive oil	2 teaspoons
spring onions (scallions)	16, trimmed to 18 cm (7 inches) long
peanuts	40 g (1½ oz/¼ cup) chopped toasted

asian rice salad

long-grain rice	400 g (14 oz/2 cups)
olive oil	2 tablespoons
red onion	1 large, finely chopped
garlic cloves	4, crushed
ginger	1 tablespoon finely chopped
red chilli	1 long, seeded and thinly sliced
spring onions (scallions)	4, finely sliced
soy sauce	2 tablespoons
sesame oil	½ teaspoon
black vinegar (see Notes)	2 teaspoons
lime juice	1 tablespoon
coriander (cilantro) leaves	2 large handfuls, roughly chopped

Trim the lamb of any excess fat and sinew. Combine the hoisin sauce, soy sauce, garlic, ginger and 1 teaspoon of the oil in a shallow dish, add the lamb and turn it so that it is well coated in the marinade. Cover the dish and refrigerate the lamb for 4 hours or overnight.

To make the rice salad, bring 1.25 litres (5 cups) of water to the boil in a large saucepan. Add the rice and cook it, uncovered, for 12–15 minutes over low heat, or until the grains are tender. Drain and rinse the rice under cold running water, then transfer it to a large bowl. While the rice is cooking, heat the oil in a frying pan over medium heat. Add the onion, garlic, ginger and chilli, and cook them for 5–6 minutes, or until the onion has softened, but not browned. Stir in the spring onion and cook for another minute. Remove the onion mixture from the heat and add it to the rice with the soy sauce, sesame oil, vinegar, lime juice and coriander, and mix well. Cover the rice salad and refrigerate until you are ready to serve.

Toss the trimmed spring onions with the remaining oil and season well. Remove the lamb from the marinade, season the meat and pour the marinade into a small saucepan. Simmer the marinade for 5 minutes, or until it is slightly reduced. Preheat the chargrill plate to medium direct heat. Cook the lamb for 5–6 minutes on each side, or until cooked to your liking, brushing it frequently with the reduced marinade, then let it rest, covered, for 3 minutes. Cook the spring onions for 1–2 minutes, or until they are tender, but still firm.

Cut the lamb across the grain into 2 cm (¾ inch) thick slices, and arrange it on a serving plate. Drizzle any juices that have been released during resting over the lamb and sprinkle it with the peanuts. Serve with the spring onions and rice salad.

Notes Black vinegar is a type of Chinese vinegar, available from Asian grocery stores. Suitable for a flat or ridged grill plate.

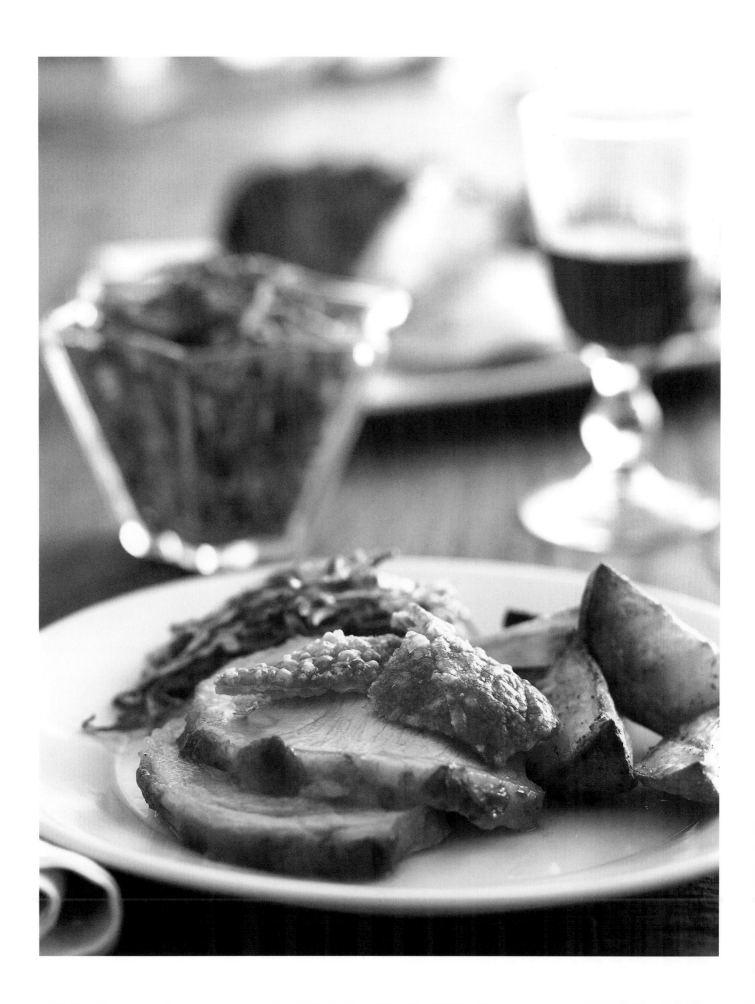

Pork loin with dill coleslaw and wedges   SERVES 6–8

coleslaw
sour cream	90 g (3 oz/⅓ cup)
horseradish	2 teaspoons prepared
lemon juice	1 tablespoon
Dijon mustard	1 tablespoon
dill	2 tablespoons finely chopped
red cabbage	300 g (11 oz/4 cups) shredded
carrots	2, peeled and grated

aniseed	1 teaspoon
apple sauce	135 g (5 oz/½ cup)
soft brown sugar	2 tablespoons
boned pork loin with skin on	1.5 kg (3 lb 5 oz)
oil	2 teaspoons
large potatoes	4, each cut into 8 wedges
olive oil	2 tablespoons
garlic salt	2 teaspoons

To make the coleslaw, put the sour cream, horseradish, lemon juice, mustard and dill in a large bowl and stir it together. Add the cabbage and carrot, toss them together well so that the coleslaw is lightly coated with dressing, and season to taste.

Dry-fry the aniseed over medium heat for 30 seconds, or until it becomes fragrant, then add the apple sauce and brown sugar, reduce the heat to low and cook, stirring, for 1 minute.

Use a sharp knife to carefully remove the skin from the pork loin. Score the skin in a diamond pattern and rub the oil and 1 tablespoon of salt over the skin, working it into the cuts. Put the potato wedges in a bowl with the olive oil and garlic salt, season them well with black pepper and toss until the wedges are well coated in oil.

Preheat a kettle or covered barbecue to medium indirect heat. Tie the pork loin with string to help it keep its shape, then put the pork and the skin in the barbecue and arrange the wedges around them. After 30 minutes, baste the pork with the apple glaze, and repeat every 10 minutes for another 30 minutes (for 1 hour cooking time in all). Turn the skin and the wedges as you go so that they cook evenly.

When the pork is ready, remove it from the barbecue and leave to rest, covered, for 10 minutes before carving. Cut the crackling with a sharp knife and arrange it on a serving platter with the pork and serve it with the wedges and coleslaw.

Note Suitable for a covered barbecue.

Stuffed calamari with lime and chilli sauce   SERVES 4

dipping sauce

lime juice	80 ml (⅓ cup)
fish sauce	60 ml (¼ cup)
palm sugar or soft brown sugar	2 tablespoons grated
red chilli	1 small, finely sliced into rounds
squid	12 medium
raw prawns (shrimp)	12, peeled, deveined, chopped
minced (ground) pork	150 g (5½ oz)
garlic cloves	4, crushed
ginger	½ teaspoon finely grated
fish sauce	3 teaspoons
lime juice	2 teaspoons
palm sugar	1 teaspoon grated
coriander (cilantro) leaves	2 tablespoons chopped
peanut oil	for brushing

To make the dipping sauce, put the lime juice, fish sauce, palm sugar and chilli in a small bowl and stir it all together until the sugar has dissolved. Cover the bowl and leave it until you are ready to eat.

Gently pull the tentacles away from the tube of the squid (the intestines should come away at the same time). Remove the quill from inside the body and throw it away, as well as any white membrane. Pull the skin away from the hood under cold running water, then cut the tentacles away from the intestines and give them a good rinse to remove the sucker rings. Finely chop the tentacles and keep them to add to the stuffing.

Put the prawns, pork, garlic, ginger, fish sauce, lime juice, palm sugar, coriander and chopped tentacles in a bowl and mix them together. Use a teaspoon to put some of the stuffing in each tube and push it to the bottom, then secure the hole with a toothpick. Take care to not overfill the tubes as the stuffing will expand when you cook them.

Preheat the chargrill plate to medium direct heat, brush the squid tubes with peanut oil, and barbecue them for 8 minutes, or until they are cooked through, turning them when the flesh becomes opaque and slightly charred. Remove the tubes from the grill, take out the toothpicks and cut each tube into 1 cm (½ inch) rounds. Serve with the dipping sauce.

Note Suitable for a flat or ridged grill plate.

Chargrilled vegetables with basil aïoli

SERVES 4

basil aïoli

garlic clove	1
basil	1 handful, torn
egg yolk	1
olive oil	125 ml (4 fl oz/½ cup)
lemon juice	2 teaspoons
red capsicums (peppers)	2 large, quartered, core and seeds removed
eggplant (aubergine)	1, cut into 5 mm (¼ inch) thick rounds
sweet potato	1 orange, peeled and cut on the diagonal into 5 mm (¼ inch) thick rounds
zucchini (courgettes)	3, sliced lengthways into 5 mm (¼ inch) thick slices
red onions	2, cut into 1 cm (½ inch) thick rounds
olive oil	80 ml (3 fl oz/⅓ cup)
Turkish bread	1 loaf, split and cut into 4 equal pieces

To make the basil aïoli, put the garlic, basil and egg yolk in the bowl of a food processor and blend until they are smooth. With the motor running, gradually add oil in a thin stream until the mixture thickens, then stir in lemon juice and season to taste. Cover and refrigerate until you are ready to dish up.

Preheat the chargrill plate to medium direct heat. Put the capsicum, skin side down, around the cool edge of the grill and cook for 8–10 minutes or until the skin is soft and blistering.

Meanwhile, brush the eggplant, sweet potato, zucchini and onion slices on both sides with olive oil and season lightly. Cook the vegetables in batches on the middle of the chargrill for 5–8 minutes, or until they are cooked through but still firm. As the vegetable pieces cook, put them on a tray in a single layer to prevent them from steaming, then grill the Turkish bread on both sides until it is lightly marked and toasted.

To assemble the burgers, spread both cut sides of the bread with 1 tablespoon of the basil aïoli and pile on some of the chargrilled vegetables. Top with the remaining toast and serve immediately.

Note Suitable for a flat or ridged grill plate.

Korean barbecue beef in lettuce leaves

SERVES 4–6

sirloin steak	600 g (1 lb 5 oz)
onion	1, grated
garlic cloves	5, crushed
Japanese soy sauce	125 ml (4 fl oz/½ cup)
sesame oil	1 teaspoon
oil	1 tablespoon
ginger	2 teaspoons finely grated
soft brown sugar	2 tablespoons
sesame seeds	1 tablespoon toasted, ground
butter lettuce	1
cooked white rice	370 g (13 oz/2 cups)
spring onions (scallions)	2, finely sliced on the diagonal
red chillies	2 small, sliced, or chilli sauce, optional

Trim any excess fat from the steak then put it in the freezer for about 45 minutes, or until it is almost frozen through. Put the onion, garlic, soy sauce, oils, ginger, sugar, ground sesame seeds and 1 teaspoon of freshly ground black pepper in a large, non-metallic bowl and stir it all together well.

Using a sharp, heavy knife cut the steak across the grain into 2–3 mm (⅛ inch) thick slices. Use a meat mallet or rolling pin to pound the meat until it is as thin as possible. Add the meat to the marinade and stir it to make sure that all of the meat is well coated in the marinade. Cover and refrigerate overnight.

Separate the lettuce leaves and put them in a large bowl with enough cold water to cover them and refrigerate.

Remove the meat and the lettuce from the refrigerator and drain the lettuce well or dry it in a salad spinner. Put the lettuce, hot rice, spring onion and chilli in separate bowls and put them on the table ready for each person to serve themself. Preheat the flat plate to high indirect heat and, working quickly, put the beef strips on the flat plate, spacing them out in a single layer, and cook for about 10 seconds on each side. Do this in two batches if your barbecue isn't large enough to fit them all at once.

To make a wrap, put some rice in the bottom of a lettuce leaf, top it with a little meat, some spring onion and chilli if you like it, then wrap the leaf around the filling and eat it immediately.

Note Suitable for a flat or ridged grill plate.

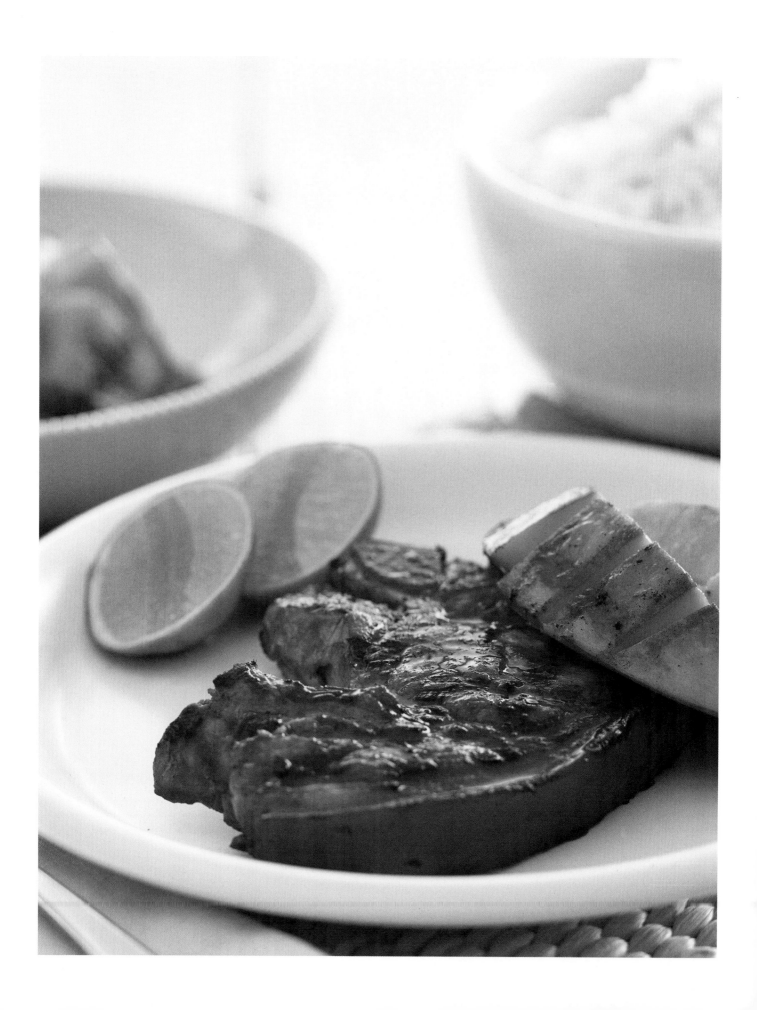

Adobo pork with coconut rice

SERVES 6

balsamic vinegar	170 ml (6 fl oz/²/₃ cup)
soy sauce	80 ml (3 fl oz/¹/₃ cup)
bay leaves	3 fresh
garlic cloves	4, crushed
pork loin chops	6 on the bone
oil	2 tablespoons
lime wedges	to serve

coconut rice

jasmine rice	400 g (14 oz/2 cups)
oil	2 tablespoons
onion	1 small, finely diced
ginger	1 teaspoon grated
garlic cloves	2, crushed
coconut milk	625 ml (2¹/₂ cups)

Put the balsamic vinegar, soy sauce, bay leaves, crushed garlic and ¹/₂ teaspoon freshly ground black pepper in a non-metallic dish and mix them all together. Add the pork chops to the marinade and turn them a few times so that they are thoroughly coated. Cover the bowl and refrigerate for at least 3 hours, or overnight.

To make the coconut rice, rinse the rice under cold, running water until the water runs clear. Heat the oil in a heavy-based saucepan over medium heat, then add the diced onion, ginger and garlic. Cook the mixture for 3 minutes, or until the onion has softened, then add the rice and stir for 1 minute, or until the rice is coated in oil. Stir in the coconut milk, bring it to the boil, then turn the heat down as low as possible and cook it very gently, covered, for 15 minutes. Remove the pan from the heat and let the rice sit for 5 minutes with the lid on, before gently fluffing it with a fork. Season well with salt and pepper.

Preheat the chargrill plate to medium direct heat. Remove the pork from the marinade and pat it dry with paper towels, then brush both sides of each chop with the oil and season them lightly with salt and pepper. Cook the chops for 8 minutes on each side, or until they are cooked through, then serve them with the coconut rice, grilled mango and lime wedges.

Note Suitable for any type of barbecue.

Grilled mangoes

mangoes	3 small
oil	2 teaspoons

Preheat the barbecue to medium direct heat.

To prepare the mango, cut each cheek straight down on either side of the stone. Score the flesh without cutting through the skin and lightly brush the cut surface with the oil.

Cook the mango on the chargrill plate, skin side down, for 2 minutes, then turn it 90 degrees and cook it for another 2 minutes to make crossed grill marks. Serve warm.

Note Suitable for a flat or ridged grill plate.

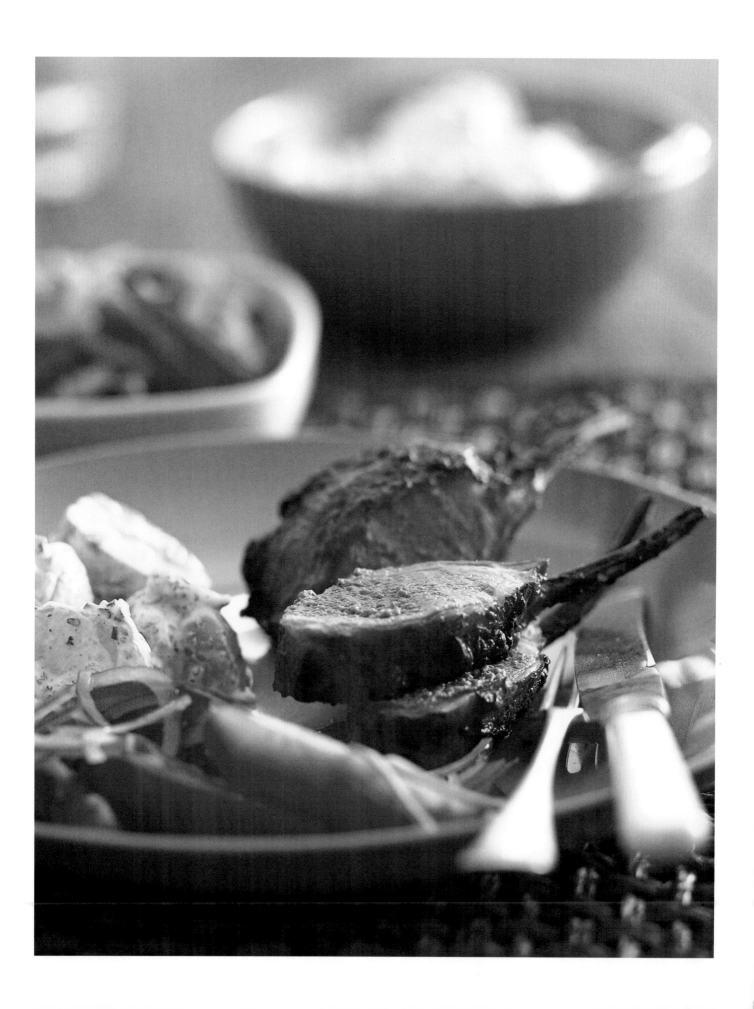

Tandoori lamb with minted potato salad   SERVES 4

tandoori paste	60 g (2 oz/¹/₄ cup)
Greek-style plain yoghurt	250 g (9 oz/1 cup)
lemon juice	1 tablespoon
racks of lamb	4 with 4–5 cutlets in each

minted potato salad

chat potatoes	600 g (1 lb 5 oz), large ones halved
Greek-style plain yoghurt	125 g (5 oz/¹/₂ cup)
Lebanese (short) cucumber	1, grated and squeezed dry
mint leaves	3 tablespoons finely chopped
garlic cloves	2, crushed

tomato and onion salsa

Roma (plum) tomatoes	6
red onion	1
lemon juice	2 tablespoons
sugar	1 teaspoon
olive oil	2 tablespoons

Combine the tandoori paste, yoghurt and lemon juice in a large, non-metallic bowl. Trim any excess fat off the racks of lamb, add to the marinade and turn them so that they are well coated. Cover and refrigerate for at least 4 hours, or overnight.

To make the minted potato salad, boil or steam the potatoes for 10 minutes, or until tender, then leave them to cool. Mix together the yoghurt, cucumber, mint and garlic and toss it through the potatoes. Season the potato salad well, cover the bowl, and refrigerate it until you are ready to dish up.

To make the tomato and onion salsa, cut the tomatoes into thin wedges, slice the onion very thinly and toss them both with the lemon juice, sugar and olive oil. Season the salsa with salt and lots of freshly cracked black pepper.

Preheat a kettle or covered barbecue to medium–high indirect heat. Cook the lamb, covered, for 10 minutes, then turn it, baste with the marinade and cook it for another 8 minutes. Leave it to rest, covered with foil, for 5 minutes. Serve the racks whole or sliced with the potato salad and tomato salsa.

Note Suitable for a covered barbecue.

Lamb fillets wrapped in vine leaves

SERVES 4

lamb fillets	12 (about 700 g/1 lb 9 oz)
lemon juice	2 teaspoons
ground cumin	1½ teaspoons
olive oil	2 tablespoons
waxy potatoes (such as pink fir apple, kifpler)	1 kg (2 lb 4 oz) waxy
vine leaves	12 large preserved in brine

avgolemono sauce

eggs	2
egg yolk	1
lemon juice	60 ml (2 fl oz/¼ cup)
chicken stock	100 ml (3 fl oz)

Trim the lamb fillets and put them in a bowl with the lemon juice, cumin and 1 tablespoon of the olive oil, then turn the fillets so they are coated. Cover the bowl and leave the lamb to marinate for 1 hour.

Steam or boil the potatoes for 10–15 minutes or until they are just tender, and when they are cool enough to handle, peel them and slice each one in half lengthways. Toss the potato halves gently in the remaining olive oil, and season.

Rinse the vine leaves under warm water, pat dry with paper towels and remove any woody stems. Lay the leaf flat with the vein side facing up, remove the lamb from the marinade, season it well with salt and pepper, and put a lamb fillet on the bottom of each vine leaf. Roll up the leaf so that it is wrapped around the lamb with the join sitting underneath.

To make the avgolemono sauce, whisk the whole eggs, egg yolk and lemon juice together, then bring the chicken stock to the boil and add 1 tablespoon of the hot stock to the egg mixture. Mix them together, then slowly add the egg mixture to the stock, stirring continuously. Cook over low heat, stirring constantly with a wooden spoon for 4–5 minutes, or until it is thick enough to hold a line drawn across the back of the spoon. Be careful to not let the sauce boil, or the mixture will curdle beyond redemption.

Preheat a barbecue to medium direct heat. Cook the potatoes on the chargrill plate for 6–7 minutes, or until they are golden and crisp and the lamb fillets for 1–2 minutes on each side for medium–rare, or until they are done to your liking.

Slice the lamb fillets in half on the diagonal and serve them with the sauce and grilled potatoes.

Note Suitable for a flat or ridged grill plate.

Yakitori chicken burger

SERVES 4

boneless, skinless chicken thighs	4, trimmed
yakitori sauce	185 ml (6 fl oz/³/₄ cup)
cornflour (cornstarch)	1 teaspoon
oil	for brushing
soft hamburger buns	4, halved
Japanese mayonnaise (see Notes)	80 g (3 oz/¹/₃ cup)
mizuna lettuce	2 handfuls
Lebanese (short) cucumber	1, ends trimmed and shaved into ribbons with a vegetable peeler

Toss the chicken fillets and yakitori sauce together in a bowl until the chicken is well coated, then cover and refrigerate for 4 hours.

Drain the sauce from the chicken into a small saucepan and sprinkle it with the cornflour. Stir the cornflour into the sauce, bring the mixture to the boil and simmer, stirring frequently, for 5 minutes, or until it is thickened, then keep it warm.

Lightly brush the chargrill with oil and preheat it to low–medium direct heat and cook the chicken on the chargrill for 6–7 minutes on each side, or until it is cooked through. Toast the burger buns for about 1 minute on each side, or until they are marked and golden.

Spread some mayonnaise on the inside surface of each bun, cover the base with mizuna and cucumber ribbons, and top with the chicken. Spread some of the thickened marinade on top of the chicken, top with the other half of the bun and then serve immediately.

Notes Japanese mayonnaise is available in larger supermarkets and Asian speciality stores. If you can't find it, use whole-egg mayonnaise instead. Suitable for any barbecue.

the perfect steak

Everybody has a preference for how they like their steak cooked and there are many variables to consider. The cut of meat, the thickness of the steak, how hot the barbecue is and the distance of the plate from the heat source are all factors contributing to how the meat will cook. These timings are approximate for a 3 cm (1¼ inch) thick steak cooked over medium –high heat.

For rare cook the steak for 2 minutes on each side. The steak should feel quite soft when pressed lightly with tongs and will be very red and moist inside.

For medium rare cook the steak for about 3 minutes on each side. The steak will still feel quite soft when gently pressed, but the internal colour will be a lighter red with pink juices.

For medium cook the steak for 4 minutes on each side or until juice comes to the surface, then turn it over and cook until juice appears on the other side. The meat will feel slightly springy to the touch and the inside will be pink in the middle and brown near the edges, with clear pink juices.

For well done cook the steak for 5 minutes on each side. Sear it until juice is pooling on top, then turn and cook until the juice is pooling again. At this stage reduce the heat slightly so that the steak can continue to cook through without burning. The steak should be quite firm when pressed, with clear juices and no sign of pink inside. A well done steak will tend to be rather dry, no matter what cut of meat is used.

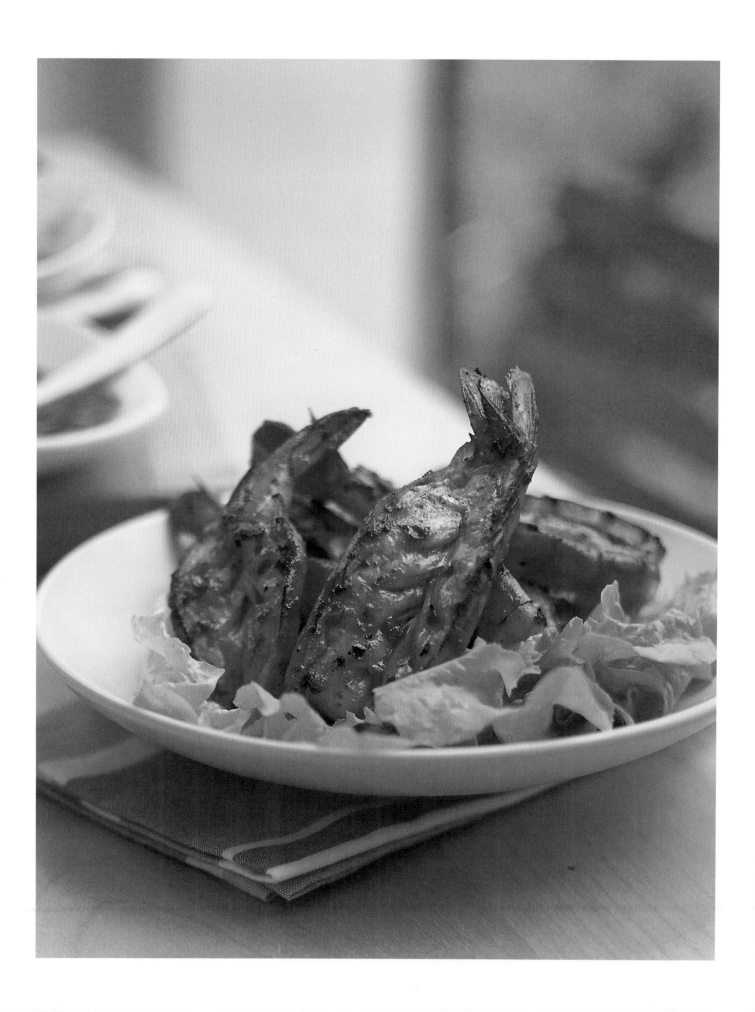

Piri piri prawns

raw prawns (shrimp)	1 kg (2 lb 4 oz) large
red chillies	4 long, seeded
white wine vinegar	185 ml (6 fl oz/³/4 cup)
garlic cloves	2 large, chopped
red chillies	6–8 small, chopped
olive oil	125 ml (4 fl oz/¹/2 cup)
mixed lettuce leaves	150 g (5 oz)

Remove the heads from the prawns and slice them down the back without cutting right through, leaving the tail intact. Open out each prawn and remove the dark vein, then store the prepared prawns in the refrigerator while you make the sauce.

To make the sauce, put the long chillies in a saucepan with the vinegar and simmer them over medium–high heat for 5 minutes, or until the chillies are soft. Let the mixture cool slightly, then put the chillies and 60 ml (2 fl oz/¹/4 cup) of the vinegar in a food processor.

Add the garlic and chopped small chillies, and blend until the mixture is smooth. While the motor is running, gradually add the oil and remaining vinegar to the food processor.

Put the prawns in the marinade, making sure they are well coated, then cover them and refrigerate for 30 minutes.

Take the prawns out of the marinade, bring the marinade to the boil and let it simmer for 5 minutes, or until it is slightly thickened and reduced. Take the prawns and the marinade out to the barbecue, and leave the saucepan with the marinade in it on the edge of the barbecue to keep warm.

Lightly oil the chargrill plate and heat it to high direct heat. Cook the prawns, basting with the marinade, for 2–3 minutes on each side, or until they are cooked through. Arrange the lettuce on four plates, top with the prawns and serve at once with the chilli sauce.

Note Suitable for a flat or ridged grill plate.

Chipolatas with quesadillas

olive oil	2 tablespoons
garlic cloves	2, crushed
crushed tomatoes	2 x 400 g (14 oz) tins
ground cumin	½ teaspoon
flour tortillas	16 x 15 cm (6 inch)
Cheddar cheese	320 g (11½ oz/2½ cups) coarsely grated
Jalapeño chillies	60 g (2 oz/⅓ cup) pickled, drained and roughly chopped
spicy chipolatas	20
coriander (cilantro) sprigs	to serve

Heat the olive oil in a frying pan over medium heat and cook the garlic for 1–2 minutes or until it is just beginning to turn golden. Add the crushed tomatoes and cumin, and season well. Reduce the heat to low and cook the relish for 30–35 minutes or until it becomes thick and pulpy.

While the relish is cooking, get to work on the quesadillas. Sprinkle a tortilla with 40 g (2½ oz/⅓ cup) of the cheese, leaving a 1 cm (½ inch) border. Scatter 1½ teaspoons of the Jalapeño chillies over the cheese and put another tortilla on top, pressing it down. Repeat with the remaining tortillas, cheese and Jalapeños until you have eight quesadillas.

Preheat the barbecue to low direct heat. Cook the chipolatas on the flat plate, turning them occasionally, for 10–12 minutes or until they are cooked through. When the chipolatas are nearly ready, start cooking the quesadillas on the chargrill for 1–2 minutes on each side, or until the cheese has melted. You may need to do this in batches, so make sure you keep them warm as you go.

Cut each quesadilla into quarters and serve them with the tomato relish and chipolatas, garnished with the coriander.

Note Suitable for any barbecue.

Grilled haloumi salad

SERVES 4

lemon juice	1½ tablespoons
mint leaves	2 tablespoons finely chopped
olive oil	125 ml (4 fl oz/½ cup)
garlic cloves	2
ciabatta bread	8 slices
haloumi cheese	300 g (11 oz), cut into 5 mm (½ inch) slices
tomatoes	3 ripe
rocket (arugula) leaves	150 g (5 oz)
pine nuts	2 tablespoons, toasted

Whisk the lemon juice, mint, 60 ml (2 fl oz/¼ cup) of the olive oil and 1 clove of crushed garlic together, and season with salt and pepper.

Brush both sides of each slice of bread with 1 tablespoon of olive oil and season well. Brush the haloumi with 1 tablespoon of olive oil, then cut the tomatoes into 1 cm (½ inch) rounds, brush each round with 1 tablespoon olive oil and season them with salt and pepper.

Preheat the barbecue to medium direct heat and chargrill the bread for 1 minute on each side, or until golden and marked, then rub on both sides with the remaining garlic. Wrap the toast in foil and keep it warm on the side of the barbecue. Chargrill the haloumi and tomato for 3–5 minutes on each side, or until browned, then drizzle with 1 tablespoon of the mint and lemon dressing.

Put the rocket leaves and pine nuts in a large bowl and add the remaining dressing. Toss salad gently until it is coated with the dressing, and pile some onto a piece of the garlic toast. Arrange some of the grilled haloumi and tomato across the top and serve it warm.

Note Suitable for a flat or ridged grill plate.

Margarita chicken with grapefruit salad   SERVES 4

chicken breasts	4, skin on, tenderloin and any excess fat removed
tequila	60 ml (2 fl oz/¼ cup)
lime juice	60 ml (2 fl oz/¼ cup)
chillies	2 small, finely chopped
garlic cloves	3, crushed
coriander (cilantro) leaves	3 tablespoons finely chopped
olive oil	1 tablespoon
lime wedges	to serve

avocado and grapefruit salad

ruby grapefruit	2
avocado	1 ripe
watercress leaves	200 g (7 oz)
French shallot	1, finely sliced
sherry vinegar	1 tablespoon
olive oil	60 ml (2 fl oz/¼ cup)

Put the chicken, tequila, lime juice, chilli, garlic, coriander and olive oil in a non-metallic bowl and mix it all together so that the chicken is coated in the marinade. Cover the bowl and refrigerate for at least 2 hours, or overnight.

Peel and segment the grapefruit, working over a bowl to save any juice for the dressing. Cut the avocado into 2 cm (¾ inch) wedges and put it in a bowl with the watercress, grapefruit and shallot. Put 1 tablespoon of the reserved grapefruit juice into a small, screw-top jar with the sherry vinegar, olive oil, salt and black pepper, and shake it up. Pour the dressing over the salad and toss it gently.

Preheat the chargrill to medium–high direct heat. Remove the chicken breasts from the marinade, season them with salt and pepper, and grill for 7–8 minutes on each side or until they are cooked through.

Slice the chicken breasts on the diagonal and serve with the salad and some lime wedges.

Note Suitable for any type of barbecue.

Garlic and mint lamb skewers

SERVES 4

lamb fillets	8, trimmed and cut into 2.5 cm (1 inch) cubes
olive oil	2 tablespoons
lemon juice	80 ml (3 fl oz/¹/₃ cup)
garlic cloves	2, crushed
mint leaves	2 teaspoons dried

yoghurt sauce

Greek-style plain yoghurt	250 g (9 oz/1 cup)
garlic clove	1, crushed

almond couscous

instant couscous	370 g (13 oz/2 cups)
olive oil	1 tablespoon
chicken stock	500 ml (17 fl oz/2 cups)
butter	40 g (1¹/₂ oz)
ras el hanout (see Notes)	2 teaspoons
currants	35 g (1 oz/¹/₄ cup), soaked in warm water for 10 minutes
slivered almonds	60 g (2 oz/¹/₂ cup), toasted
mint leaves	2 large handfuls, chopped

Put the lamb in a non-metallic bowl with the oil, lemon juice, garlic and mint. Stir the pieces around so that they are well coated and season with black pepper. Cover and refrigerate for at least 4 hours, or overnight.

Make the yoghurt sauce by mixing the yoghurt and garlic in a small bowl, then refrigerate it until you are ready to use it.

Put the couscous in a heatproof bowl, drizzle it with the olive oil and season well with salt. Bring the chicken stock to the boil and pour it over the couscous, then cover the bowl and leave it for 10 minutes to absorb the stock. Add the butter and fluff it through with a fork until the butter has melted and the grains are separated. Stir in the ras el hanout, currants, almonds and mint, and season to taste with salt and pepper.

Soak eight wooden skewers in cold water for 1 hour, then thread the lamb onto them and season well. Preheat the barbecue to medium–high direct heat and grill the skewers for 3–4 minutes on each side, or until they are cooked to your liking. Serve the skewers on a bed of couscous with the yoghurt sauce.

Notes Ras el hanout is a fragrant spice blend used in Moroccan cooking and is available from specialist food stores. If you can't find it, you can make your own (see the recipe on page 65). Suitable for any type of barbecue.

Chinese-style barbecue spareribs

SERVES 6

hoisin sauce	60 ml (2 fl oz/¼ cup)
oyster sauce	80 ml (3 fl oz/⅓ cup)
rice wine	2 tablespoons
soy sauce	125 ml (4 fl oz/½ cup)
garlic cloves	6, crushed
ginger	3 teaspoons finely grated
American-style pork ribs	2 kg (4 lb 8 oz)
honey	2 tablespoons

Mix the hoisin sauce, oyster sauce, rice wine, soy sauce, garlic and ginger in a large, non-metallic bowl, add the ribs and turn them so that they are coated in the marinade. Cover the bowl and refrigerate for at least 4 hours, or overnight.

Remove the ribs from the marinade and tip the marinade into a small saucepan with the honey. Simmer the mixture over low heat for 5 minutes, or until it becomes slightly syrupy — you will be using this to baste the ribs as they cook.

Heat a kettle or covered barbecue to medium indirect heat and cook the ribs, covered, for 10 minutes, then turn and cook them for another 5 minutes. Continue cooking, basting and turning the ribs frequently for 30 minutes, or until they are cooked through and caramelized all over.

Once the ribs are cooked, let them rest, covered, for 10 minutes.

Cut the racks into individual ribs to serve and make sure there are plenty of napkins available — these ribs should be eaten with your fingers and are quite sticky.

Note Suitable for a covered barbecue.

Beef fajitas

rump steak	800 g (1 lb 12 oz)
cumin	2 teaspoons
ground oregano	1 teaspoon
paprika	1 teaspoon
Worcestershire sauce	2 tablespoons
soy sauce	1 tablespoon
garlic cloves	3
lime juice	60 ml (2 fl oz/¼ cup)
onion	1 large, thinly sliced
red capsicum (pepper)	1, cut into 5 mm (¼ inch) strips
green capsicum (pepper)	1, cut into 5 mm (¼ inch) strips
olive oil	1 tablespoon
flour tortillas	8
avocado	1 ripe, diced
Roma (plum) tomatoes	2 ripe, diced
Cheddar cheese	60 g (2 oz/½ cup) grated
sour cream	90 g (3 oz/⅓ cup)

Trim the steak of any fat and give it a good pounding with a meat mallet on both sides. Mix the cumin, oregano, paprika, Worcestershire sauce, soy sauce, garlic and lime juice in a shallow, non-metallic dish and add the beef. Turn the meat so it is well coated in the marinade, then cover and refrigerate for at least 4 hours, or overnight.

Drain the steak, reserving the marinade, and pat it dry with paper towels. Put the marinade in a small saucepan, bring it to the boil and simmer it over medium heat for 5 minutes, or until it is reduced by about half, and keep it warm.

Preheat a barbecue to high direct heat. Toss the onion and capsicum with the oil then spread them across the flat plate, turning every so often for 10 minutes, or until they are cooked through and caramelized. While the vegetables are cooking, grill the steak on the chargrill plate for 3 minutes on each side, or until cooked to your liking, then remove it from the heat and let it rest, covered, for 5 minutes.

Thinly slice the steak and arrange it on a plate with the onion and capsicum strips and serve them with the tortillas, avocado, tomato, cheese, sour cream and marinade sauce. Let everyone fill their own tortillas with some of each ingredient.

Note Suitable for a flat or ridged grill plate.

Thai red chicken with Asian greens

SERVES 4

red curry paste	1 tablespoon
coconut cream	250 g (9 oz/1 cup)
kaffir lime leaves	3
boneless chicken breasts	4, skin on, tenderloin removed
jasmine rice	400 g (14 oz/2 cups)
chicken stock	250 ml (9 fl oz/1 cup)
soy sauce	1 tablespoon
garlic clove	1, bruised
ginger	2 x 2 cm (¾ x ¾ inch) piece, bruised
Chinese broccoli	750 g (1 lb /1o oz), washed and tied in a bunch
coriander (cilantro) sprigs	to serve

Combine curry paste, coconut cream and kaffir lime leaves, then add chicken and turn it so that it is coated in marinade. Cover bowl and refrigerate it for at least 4 hours, or overnight.

Half an hour before you are ready to cook the chicken, wash the rice in a sieve until the water runs clear. Put the rice in a saucepan with 750 ml (3 cups) water and bring to the boil for 1 minute. Cover the saucepan with a tightly fitting lid, reduce the heat to as low as possible and let it cook for 1o minutes. Without removing the lid, remove the pan from the heat and leave it for at least 1o minutes, or until you are ready to eat. Meanwhile, bring the chicken stock, soy sauce, garlic and ginger to the boil in a small saucepan for 5 minutes, or until reduced by half. Strain the mixture, return the liquid to the saucepan and keep it warm.

Bring a large saucepan of salted water to the boil and add the Chinese broccoli, stalk side down. Cook for 2–3 minutes or until just tender, then drain well and arrange it on a serving dish. Just before serving, pour the hot chicken stock mixture over the greens.

Preheat the flat grill plate to medium direct heat. Cook the chicken, skin side down first, for 7–8 minutes on each side, or until it is cooked through. Transfer the chicken to a plate, cover it loosely with foil and leave it to rest. Fluff the rice with a fork and put it in a serving bowl. Serve the chicken with the rice and green, garnished with coriander sprigs.

Note Suitable for a flat or ridged grill plate.

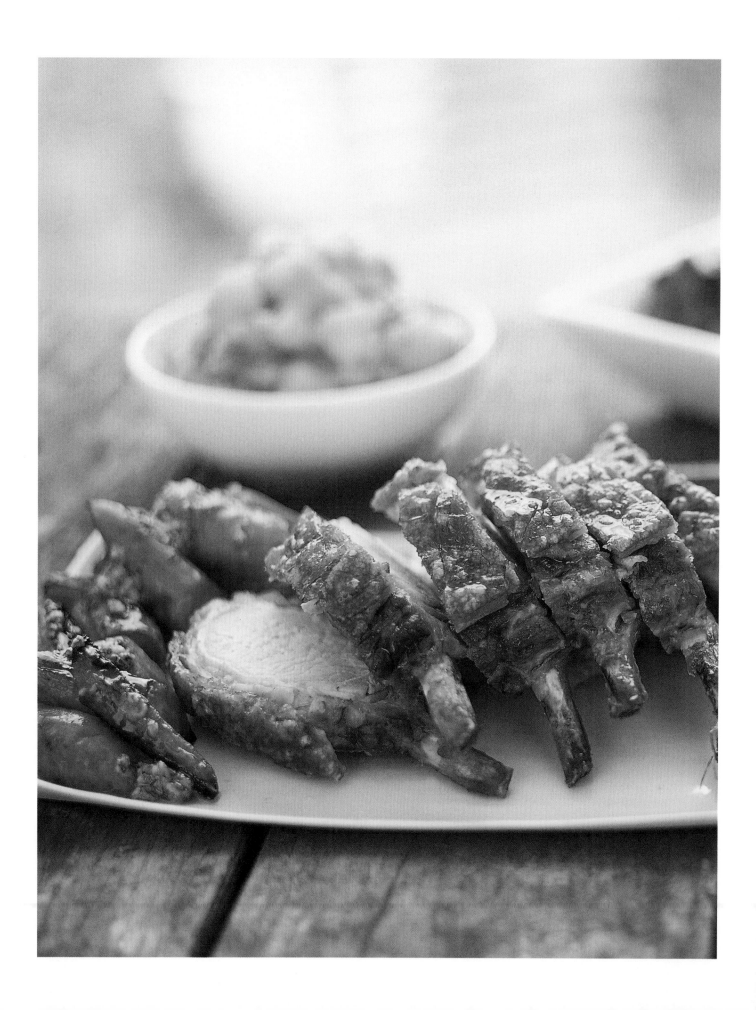

Roast rack of pork with apple sauce

SERVES 6

Granny Smith apples	6
sugar	90 g (3 oz/¹/₃ cup)
white vinegar	60 ml (2 fl oz/¹/₄ cup)
mint leaves	2 tablespoons finely shredded
rack of pork	1 with 6 ribs (about 1.6 kg/ 3 lb 8 oz)
olive oil	1 tablespoon

roasted vegetables

orange sweet potatoes	2
pumpkin	1 kg (2 lb 4 oz) piece
onions	12 small
carrots	6
olive oil	80 ml (3 fl oz/¹/₃ cup)
garlic cloves	6, unpeeled
flat-leaf (Italian) parsley	2 tablespoons finely chopped

Peel the apples, remove the seeds, and roughly dice the flesh. Simmer them over low heat with the sugar, vinegar and 60 ml (2 fl oz/¹/₄ cup) water in a small saucepan for 15 minutes, or until they are cooked through and just beginning to collapse. Remove the sauce from the heat and stir in the shredded mint.

Score the skin on the rack of pork in a large diamond pattern, rub the oil all over the pork, then rub 1 teaspoon salt into the skin. To make the roast vegetables, peel the sweet potato, pumpkin, onions and carrots, and cut them into large, even pieces. Gently toss the vegetables with 2 tablespoons of olive oil until they are coated, and season them well with salt and freshly ground black pepper.

Trim the root end from the garlic cloves, drizzle ¹/₂ teaspoon of oil over them and wrap them in a double layer of foil.

Preheat a kettle or covered barbecue to medium indirect heat. Put the pork rack in the middle of the barbecue, cover it and roast for 1 hour 20 minutes, or until the juices run clear when a skewer is inserted into the thickest part of the flesh. When the pork has been cooking for about 20 minutes, arrange the vegetables around the roast and cook, covered, for 1 hour or until golden and tender. Add the garlic to the barbecue and cook it for 30 minutes or until it has softened.

When the garlic cloves are cool enough to handle, squeeze them from their skin, mash them with the remaining olive oil and stir in the parsley. Season with salt and pepper, and drizzle the dressing over the roast vegetables just before serving.

When the pork is cooked, remove from the barbecue, and leave it to rest, covered, for 10 minutes. Slice between the bones and serve it with the roasted vegetables and chunky apple sauce.

Note Suitable for a covered barbecue.

Roast sirloin with mustard pepper crust   SERVES 6–8

Dijon mustard	90 g (3 oz/¹⁄₃ cup)
light soy sauce	2 tablespoons
plain (all-purpose) flour	2 tablespoons
olive oil	60 ml (2 fl oz/¹⁄₄ cup)
thyme leaves	3 teaspoons chopped
garlic cloves	4, crushed
sirloin	2.5 kg (5 lb 8 oz) piece, trimmed but with the fat still on top
potatoes	6
butter	2 tablespoons, melted
onion	1, roughly diced
carrot	1 large, roughly diced
celery stalks	2, roughly chopped
red wine	250 ml (9 fl oz/1 cup)
beef stock	500 ml (17 fl oz/2 cups)
bay leaves	2
cornflour (cornstarch)	2 teaspoons
asparagus	500 g (1 lb 2 oz)
olive oil	2 tablespoons

Mix the mustard, soy sauce, flour, 2 tablespoons of the olive oil, 2 teaspoons of thyme, two crushed garlic cloves and 1 tablespoon of cracked black pepper in a small bowl.

Coat the sirloin with the mustard mixture, put it on a wire rack over a tray and refrigerate it for 1 hour so the crust sets.

To make hasselback potatoes, boil the potatoes in their skins for 10–12 minutes, or until they are just cooked. Once they are cool enough to handle, peel and cut them in half lengthways. Make small even slices across the top of the potato, cutting only two-thirds of the way down, brush each one liberally with butter and season them well with salt and pepper.

Heat emaining olive oil in a large saucepan, add onion, carrot, celery and the remaining garlic, and cook them for 5 minutes. Pour in red wine, cook for another 5 minutes, then add the beef stock, bay leaves and remaining thyme. Mix the cornflour with 1 tablespoon water until it is smooth and add it to pan. Simmer the sauce over low heat for 20 minutes, or until it is slightly thickened, then strain and season to taste with salt and pepper.

Preheat a kettle or covered barbecue to medium indirect heat, put the sirloin in the middle of the barbecue and arrange the potatoes arround it. Replace the cover and cook for 45 minutes.

Remove sirloin from barbecue, and leave it to rest, covered, for 10 minutes before carving. Serve the steak with the hasselback potatoes, asparagus and red wine sauce.

To make the grilled asparagus, trim the woody ends from the asparagus, toss them with olive oil and season well with salt and pepper. Cook on a preheated chargrill plate, covered, for 5 minutes, or until cooked through.

Note Suitable for a covered barbecue.

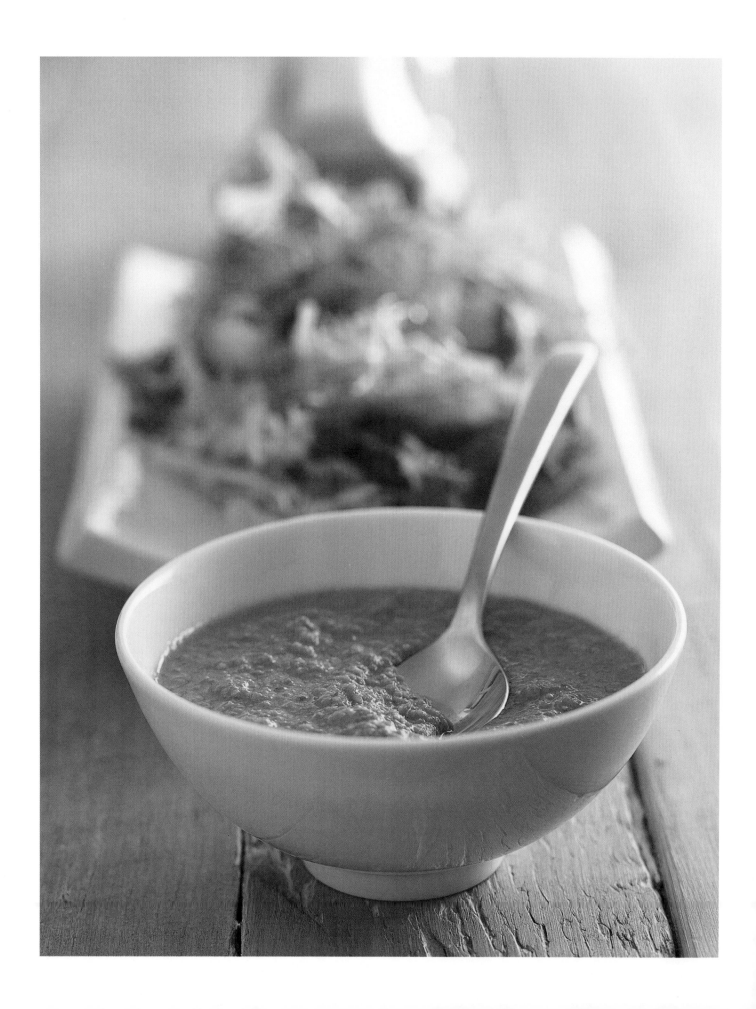

three ways with sauces

To turn a basic meal into something impressive can be as straightforward as making a simple sauce. Some sauces can be made ahead and stored in the refrigerator for a couple of days; others need to be used straightaway. The ones given below are perfect for barbecued food and can be used with a variety of produce and, while a little labour-intensive, are well worth the effort...and so much bigger on flavour than any shop-bought equivalent.

ROMESCO SAUCE

Preheat the barbecue to medium direct heat. Mix 2 tablespoons olive oil with $1/4$ teaspoon paprika, add 1 small, seeded and quartered capsicum, 3 ripe Roma (plum) tomatoes and 2 long red chillies, and toss. Cook the capsicum and tomatoes on the chargrill plate for 5 minutes, then add the chillies and cook for another 5 minutes or until the tomatoes are softened and the vegetables are charred. Peel the capsicum and tomatoes when they are cool, then remove the seeds and skin from the chilli. Process 50 g (2 oz/$1/3$ cup) blanched and toasted almonds and hazelnuts until they are finely ground. Add the vegetables, 3 crushed cloves garlic, 1 tablespoon red wine vinegar and 1 tablespoon lemon juice, and blend to a paste. Slowly add another 2 tablespoons olive oil and season to taste. If the sauce is too thick, add 2 tablespoons of water to get it to a pouring consistency. Serve with barbecued seafood.

SKORDALIA

Peel 500 g (1 lb 2 oz) floury potatoes and cut into small cubes. Cook in boiling water for 10 minutes, or until very soft. Drain the potato and mash until smooth. Stir in 5 crushed garlic cloves, 1 teaspoon salt and a pinch of white pepper. Gradually pour in 185 ml (6 fl oz/$3/4$ cup) olive oil, mixing well with a wooden spoon. Add 2 tablespoons white vinegar and season with additional salt and ground white pepper, if needed. Serve as a sauce with barbecued meat, seafood or chicken.

BARBECUE SAUCE

Heat 2 teaspoons oil in a small pan over low heat and cook 1 finely chopped small onion for 3 minutes, or until soft. Add 1 tablespoon malt vinegar, 1 tablespoon soft brown sugar, 1 tablespoon Worcestershire sauce and 80 ml ($2^3/4$ fl oz/$1/3$ cup) tomato sauce and bring to the boil. Reduce the heat and simmer for 3 minutes, stirring occasionally. Serve warm or at room temperature. Can be kept, covered and refrigerated, for up to a week. Serve with burgers or barbecued meat.

romesco sauce

Spanish-style seafood salad

SERVES 4

Balmain bugs (slipper lobsters)	8 raw
raw king prawns (jumbo shrimp)	1 kg (2 lb 4 oz)
baby squid tubes	500 g (1 lb 2 oz), cleaned
olive oil	125 ml (4 fl oz/½ cup)
garlic cloves	3, finely chopped
basil leaves	3 tablespoons chopped
lemon juice	80 ml (3 fl oz/⅓ cup)
rocket (arugula) leaves	150 g (5 oz)
frisée lettuce	150 g (5 oz)
extra virgin olive oil	2 tablespoons
red wine vinegar	1 tablespoon
Romesco sauce (page 141)	1 quantity

To prepare the bugs, cut into the membrane where the head and body join, then twist off the tail and discard the head. Use kitchen scissors to cut down both sides of the underside shell, working the scissors between the flesh and shell, then peel back the undershell and throw it away. To prepare the prawns, remove the heads and legs, leaving the shells and tails intact. Turn each prawn on its back and cut a slit through the centre of each prawn lengthways, taking care not to cut all the way through. Open out the prawn to form a butterfly and remove the dark vein from the back, starting at the head end. Wash the squid and pat them dry with paper towels, then cut a small slit in the base of the tubes so that they open up when cooking.

Mix together the oil, garlic, basil and lemon juice in a large bowl, add the seafood and toss so that it is coated in the marinade. Cover the bowl and refrigerate it for 30 minutes.

Just before you cook the seafood, toss the salad leaves with the olive oil and vinegar, and refrigerate, covered, until you are ready to eat.

Heat the barbecue chargrill plate to very high direct heat. Cook the bugs for 5–6 minutes, or until the shells turn pink and the flesh starts pulling away from the shells. Halfway through cooking the bugs, add the prawns and cook them, flesh side down, for 2–3 minutes. Turn and cook for another 2–3 minutes, or until they are pink and cooked through. Add the squid after turning the prawns, and cook them for 1–2 minutes, or until they are brown, marked and just cooked through. Remove all of the seafood from the barbecue as soon as it is just done, as residual heat will continue to cook the meat. Arrange the salad leaves on a serving plate, top them with the barbecued seafood and drizzle with Romesco sauce. Serve the salad immediately, with any remaining Romesco sauce on the side and crusty bread rolls to soak up all of the juices.

Note Suitable for a flat or ridged grill plate.

Stuffed eggplant

eggplants (aubergines)	2
olive oil	2 tablespoons
onion	1, chopped
garlic cloves	2, crushed
tomatoes	4, roughly chopped
tomato paste (concentrated purée)	2 teaspoons
dill	2 tablespoons chopped
flat-leaf (Italian) parsley	2 tablespoons chopped
currants	2 tablespoons
pine nuts	2 tablespoons
red wine vinegar	1 tablespoons
kefalotyri cheese	150 g (5 oz/1½ cups) finely grated

Cut each eggplant in half lengthways and use a sharp knife to cut out the flesh, leaving a 5 mm (¼ inch) thick shell. Finely dice the flesh, toss it with 2 teaspoons of salt and drain it in a colander over a bowl for 30 minutes. Squeeze out any excess moisture from the eggplant, rinse under cold water and drain well on paper towels.

Heat 1 tablespoon oil in a frying pan over high heat. Add the diced eggplant and cook, stirring frequently, for 5 minutes, or until it is browned, then put it in a large bowl. Heat the remaining oil in the frying pan over medium heat, cook the onion and garlic for 2 minutes, then add the tomato, tomato paste, dill, parsley, currants, pine nuts and vinegar. Stir it all together and cook it for 8–1o minutes, stirring occasionally. Add the tomato mixture to the eggplant with 50 g (2 oz/1 cup) of the kefalotyri, season with black pepper and mix well.

Spoon the vegetable mixture into the eggplant shells and sprinkle the remaining cheese over the top. Preheat a kettle or covered barbecue to medium indirect heat and put the stuffed eggplants in the middle of the barbecue, cover them and cook for 30 minutes, or until they are cooked through. This vegetarian treat is delicious with a green salad.

Note Suitable for a covered barbecue.

Honey mustard chicken with onion mash   SERVES 4–6

honey	175 g (6 oz/½ cup)
Dijon mustard	60 g (2 oz/¼ cup)
oil	2 tablespoons
white wine vinegar	2 tablespoons
garlic cloves	3, crushed
parsley leaves	2 tablespoons chopped
chicken	1 x 1.8 kg (4 lb), cut into 10 serving pieces

spring onion mash

potatoes	1 kg (2 lb 4 oz) floury (starchy)
butter	2 tablespoons
milk	80 ml (3 fl oz/⅓ cup)
cream	60 ml (2 fl oz/¼ cup)
spring onions (scallions)	3, finely sliced

Put the honey, mustard, oil, white wine vinegar, garlic, parsley and ¼ teaspoon freshly ground black pepper in a large, non-metallic bowl. Mix it all together well, and put aside 60 ml (2 fl oz/¼ cup) of the marinade to baste the chicken during cooking. Add the chicken pieces to the rest of the marinade and turn them so that they are thoroughly coated. Cover the bowl and refrigerate it for at least 4 hours, or overnight.

To make the spring onion mash, peel the potatoes and cut into large chunks. Steam or boil the pieces for 12 minutes, or until they are tender, then drain the water away and briefly return potato to the heat, shaking the pan, to dry any excess moisture. Add the butter, milk and cream, and mash the potato until smooth and lump-free. Stir in the spring onion, season to taste and keep the potato warm while you cook the chicken.

Preheat a covered or kettle barbecue to medium indirect heat and cook the chicken pieces for 20–30 minutes, or until they are cooked through. The breast pieces may take as little as 15 minutes, while dark meat will take longer. Baste the chicken with the marinade during the last 5–8 minutes of cooking, but no earlier or it is likely to burn. Serve the chicken on a bed of spring onion mash.

Note Suitable for a covered barbecue.

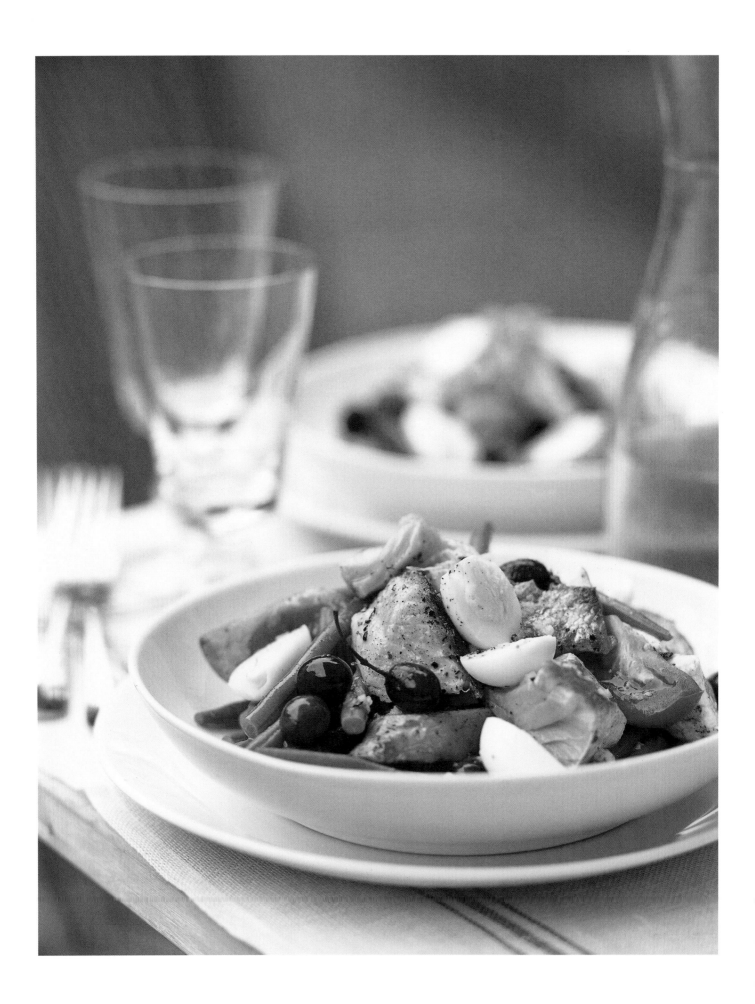

Crispy-skinned salmon salad niçoise

SERVES 4

kipfler potatoes	400 g (14 oz), washed
olive oil	1 tablespoon
sea salt	to taste
quail eggs	12
green beans	300 g (11 oz) small
olive oil	2 teaspoons, extra
salmon fillets	3 x 200 g (7 oz)
ripe tomatoes	2 large, cut into 8 wedges
black olives	150 g (5 oz) small
extra virgin olive oil	80 ml (3 fl oz/⅓ cup)
white wine vinegar	1½ tablespoons
lemon juice	1 tablespoon
garlic cloves	2, crushed

Boil or steam the potatoes for about 1o minutes or until they are almost cooked through. Drain and cut into 2 cm (¾ inch) slices on the diagonal, then toss them with the olive oil until they are coated and season to taste with sea salt.

Put the eggs in a saucepan of cold water and bring them to the boil for 2 minutes. Cool the eggs under running water, then peel and halve them. Bring the water back to the boil and cook the beans for 2 minutes or until they are just tender, then drain them, plunge them into cold water and drain again.

Heat the barbecue to medium–high direct heat. Cook the potato slices on the chargrill plate for 2 minutes on each side, or until golden and cooked through. Brush the salmon fillets with the extra oil and cook, skin side down, on the flat plate for 2–3 minutes, then turn and cook for another 2–3 minutes, or until they are almost cooked through. The salmon should be slightly rare in the middle. Break the fillets into chunks with a fork, removing any bones as you go.

Put the potato in a large bowl with the beans, tomato and olives. Whisk together the oil, vinegar, lemon juice and garlic, and add the dressing to the bowl. Season with sea salt and freshly ground black pepper, and gently toss the salad until well combined. Pile some of the potato mixture on serving plates, top with the salmon and eggs, and serve immediately.

Note Suitable for a flat or ridged grill plate.

Chilli beef burger with pineapple salsa

SERVES 4

burgers

minced (ground) beef	500 g (1 lb 2 oz)
Asian shallots	6, finely chopped
crisp fried onion flakes (see Notes)	25 g (1 oz/¼ cup)
garlic cloves	3, finely chopped
red chillies	2 long, seeded, finely chopped
coriander (cilantro) leaves (include some stems)	4 tablespoons finely chopped
chilli garlic sauce (see Notes)	2–2½ tablespoons
egg	1, lightly beaten
fresh breadcrumbs	160 g (5 oz/2 cups)

pineapple mint salsa

pineapple	1 small ripe
palm sugar or soft brown sugar	1 tablespoon grated
red chilli	1 small, seeded and finely diced
rice vinegar	½ teaspoon
lime juice	2 tablespoons
spring onions (scallions)	4, finely chopped
mint leaves	3 tablespoons chopped
olive oil	for brushing
Turkish bread	1 loaf, cut into 4 pieces, or 4 round Turkish rolls
mignonette or green oak lettuce leaves	3 handfuls

To make the burgers, put the mince, shallots, onion flakes, garlic, chilli, coriander, chilli garlic sauce, egg, breadcrumbs and 1½ teaspoons of salt in a large bowl, and knead it well with your hands, working the ingredients through until they are thoroughly combined. Cover the bowl and refrigerate it for 2 hours.

Meanwhile, to make the pineapple salsa, peel the pineapple, remove all of the eyes and slice it lengthways into quarters. Remove the central core and cut the flesh into 1 cm (½ inch) dice. Put the pineapple in a non-metallic mixing bowl with the remaining salsa ingredients and stir them together, then cover the bowl and refrigerate for 1 hour to let the flavours develop.

Using wet hands, divide the mince mixture into four equal portions, roll each portion into a ball, then flatten it slightly to form patties. When you are ready to cook the burgers, preheat the chargrill plate to medium direct heat. Lightly brush the patties with oil and grill for 5–6 minutes, then flip them and cook for another 5–6 minutes, or until they are well browned and cooked through. A few minutes before the patties are ready, toast the bread, cut side down, on the chargrill plate for 1–2 minutes, or until it is marked and golden.

To assemble the burgers, divide the lettuce among four of the toasted bread slices. Add a pattie and top with the pineapple and mint salsa. Season the burgers with salt and pepper, then top with the remaining toasted bread and serve immediately.

Notes Crisp-fried onion flakes and chilli garlic sauce are available from Asian grocery stores. Suitable for any barbecue.

Rosemary lamb on grilled polenta

SERVES 4

lamb fillets	600 g (1 lb 5 oz)
rosemary	1 tablespoon finely chopped
garlic cloves	3, bruised
olive oil	2 tablespoons
lemon juice	1 tablespoon
instant polenta	250 g (9 oz/1²/₃ cups)
Parmesan cheese	35 g (1 oz/¹/₃ cup) grated
butter	20 g (1 oz)
rocket (arugula) leaves	60 g (2 oz/1¹/₂ cups)

anchovy and rosemary sauce

anchovy fillets	8 large, chopped
rosemary	3 teaspoons finely chopped
olive oil	150 ml (5 fl oz)
lemon juice	1 tablespoon

Trim the lamb fillets of any fat and sinew, and put them in a non-metallic bowl with the rosemary, garlic, olive oil and lemon juice, turning the fillets until they are well coated. Season with pepper, cover the bowl and refrigerate it for at least 4 hours, or overnight.

Meanwhile, to make the polenta, bring 1 litre of salted water to the boil in a heavy-based saucepan. Whisking constantly, add the polenta in a thin stream and stir until it thickens and starts to come away from the side of the pan. Remove the pan from the heat and add the Parmesan and butter, then season generously with salt and freshly ground black pepper. Stir the polenta until the cheese and butter have melted, then pour it into a lightly greased 22 cm (9 inch) square baking tin and smooth the surface. Refrigerate the polenta for 2 hours or until it is cool and firm, then turn it out onto a chopping board, trim the edges and cut the block into four squares.

While the polenta is cooling, make the anchovy and rosemary sauce. Put the anchovies and rosemary in a food processor and blend them to a paste. Add the olive oil in a thin stream, then add the lemon juice and season to taste.

Preheat the chargrill plate to medium direct heat. Grill the polenta squares for 7–8 minutes on each side or until they are crisp and golden. When the polenta is ready, move the squares to the side of the grill, season the lamb fillets with salt and cook them for 2–3 minutes on each side for medium–rare, or until they are cooked to your liking.

To serve, slice the lamb fillets into four pieces on the diagonal, cutting across the grain. Put the grilled polenta on warmed serving plates, top it with the lamb and rocket and drizzle with the sauce.

Note Suitable for any type of barbecue.

Five-spice roast chicken

chicken	1.8 kg (4 lb)
soy sauce	1 tablespoon
garlic cloves	2, crushed
ginger	1 teaspoon finely grated
honey	1 tablespoon
rice wine	1 tablespoon
five-spice	1 teaspoon
peanut oil	1 tablespoon

Wash the chicken and pat it thoroughly dry inside and out with paper towels. Whisk the soy sauce, garlic, ginger, honey, rice wine and five-spice together in a small bowl and brush it all over the chicken, ensuring every bit of skin is well coated. Put the chicken on a wire rack over a baking tray and refrigerate it, uncovered, for at least 8 hours, or overnight.

Preheat a kettle or covered barbecue to medium indirect heat and put a drip tray under the rack. Brush the chicken liberally with the peanut oil and put it breast side up in the middle of the barbecue over the drip tray. Cover the barbecue and roast the chicken for 1 hour 10 minutes, or until the juices run clear when you pierce it with a skewer between the thigh and body. Check the chicken every so often, and if it appears to be over-browning, cover it loosely with foil. Leave it to rest, covered, for 10 minutes before carving and serving. The flavours in this style of chicken go particularly well with steamed Asian greens and fried rice.

Note Suitable for a covered barbecue.

Lobster with burnt butter sauce and lemon   SERVES 8

butter	150 g (5 oz)
lemon juice	60 ml (2 fl oz/¼ cup)
flat-leaf (Italian) parsley	2 tablespoons chopped
garlic clove	1 small, crushed
lobster tails	8 in the shell
lemons	2, cut into wedges

Melt the butter in a small saucepan over medium heat and cook it for 3 minutes or until it begins to brown, but watch it carefully to make sure that it doesn't burn. Lower the heat, and cook the butter for another 2 minutes, or until it is a dark, golden brown. Remove the pan from the heat, add the lemon juice, parsley and garlic, and season with salt and freshly ground black pepper.

Cut the lobster tails lengthways and remove any digestive tract, but leave the meat in the shell. Preheat the chargrill plate to medium direct heat and brush the lobster meat with lots of the butter mixture. Cook the lobster tails, cut side down, on the chargrill plate for 6 minutes, then turn them over and cook for another 3–5 minutes, or until the shells turn bright red. While the lobster is cooking, put the lemon wedges on the hottest part of the chargrill and cook them for 1 minute on each side, or until they are marked and heated through. Arrange the lobster on a serving plate and serve it with the grilled lemon wedges and the rest of the warm brown butter as a dipping sauce. This is delicious with a green salad and some crusty bread to soak up the juices.

Note Suitable for any type of barbecue.

three ways with salsa

Salsas are refreshing little dishes that have something of a split personality. They can be a side dish, a sauce or a dip or a bit of a combination of all three. They can be made with numerous ingredients, such as vegetables, fruit and cheese, which are usually cut into very small pieces or roughly puréed. Choose a combination that complement the main dish. They are mostly served at room temperature. Salsas are commonly used in Mexican, Spanish and Italian cuisine.

TOMATO SALSA

Combine 4 finely diced ripe tomatoes, 40 g ($1^{1}/_{2}$ oz/$^{1}/_{4}$ cup) finely chopped red onion, 1 large handful chopped coriander (cilantro) and 1 tablespoon lime juice. Season to taste, then cover the salsa with plastic wrap and refrigerate. Remove the salsa from the refrigerator 15 minutes before you are ready to use it so the ingredients have time to return to room temperature and their full flavour.

BOCCONCINI, TOMATO AND SUN-DRIED CAPSICUM SALSA

Combine 180 g (6 oz) diced bocconcini, 60 g (2 oz/$^{1}/_{3}$ cup) drained, chopped sun-dried capsicum in oil and 1 finely sliced spring onion (scallion). Whisk together 1 tablespoon extra virgin olive oil and 2 teaspoons red wine vinegar until thoroughly blended. Stir through 1 tablespoon shredded basil and 1 tablespoon flat-leaf parsley. Toss the dressing through the bocconcini and tomato mixture and season well with salt and pepper. Serve at room temperature with barbecued steak or tuna.

MANGO AND AVOCADO SALSA

Peel 1 large ripe mango and dice the flesh. Peel 1 large ripe avocado and dice the flesh. Mix the mango and avocado together, along with 1 finely chopped spring onion (scallion), 1 tablespoon lime juice and a dash of Tabasco sauce. Serve at room temperature, or chilled, with steak, chicken or prawns (shrimp).

tomato salsa

Chilli bean tortilla wraps

chilli beans

olive oil	2 tablespoons
garlic cloves	2, crushed
onion	1, finely chopped
capsicum (pepper)	1 green, seeded, cored and chopped
red chillies	2 small, seeded and finely chopped
cayenne pepper	½ teaspoon
paprika	1 teaspoon
ground cumin	1 teaspoon
sugar	¼ teaspoon
crushed tomatoes	440 g (15 oz) tin
red kidney beans	440 g (15 oz) tin, drained and rinsed
tomato paste (concentrated purée)	1 tablespoon
flour tortillas	12 x 20 cm (8 inch) soft
Cheddar cheese	225 g (8 oz/1¾ cups), coarsely grated
sour cream	250 g (9 oz/1 cup)
coriander (cilantro) sprigs	to garnish
lime	1, cut into 8 wedges

To make the chilli beans, heat the oil in a saucepan over low heat and cook the garlic, onion and capsicum, stirring frequently, for 8–10 minutes, or until the onion and capsicum have softened. Add the chilli, cayenne pepper, paprika, cumin, sugar, tomato, beans, tomato paste and 125 ml (4 fl oz/½ cup) water. Bring the mixture to the boil, then reduce the heat and simmer for 15–20 minutes, or until thickened and reduced. Season to taste.

To assemble the wraps, put some of the chilli beans along the middle of each tortilla, sprinkle it with 2 tablespoons of the cheese and roll it up. Put three rolls, seam side down, on a double layer of foil and seal the foil to form a parcel. Preheat the flat plate to low–medium direct heat and grill the parcels for 6–8 minutes on each side or until they are heated through.

Unwrap the foil parcels and slide the tortillas onto serving plates. Top with the guacamole, sour cream and salsa, garnish with coriander sprigs and serve them with the lime wedges.

Note Suitable for any type of barbecue.

Pork in green ginger wine marinade

pork fillets	800 g (1 lb 12 oz), trimmed
ginger	1 tablespoon finely grated
garlic cloves	2, finely chopped
preserved ginger in syrup	1 tablespoon finely chopped
green ginger wine (see Notes)	60 ml (2 fl oz/¼ cup)
kecap manis	2½ tablespoons
sesame oil	½ teaspoon
oil	1 tablespoon
bulb spring onions	8, green parts removed, quartered
olive oil	1 tablespoon
coriander (cilantro) sprigs	to serve

Cut the pork fillets into 12 cm x 2.5 cm (5 inch x 1 inch) strips and put them in a non-metallic bowl with the ginger, garlic, preserved ginger, green ginger wine, kecap manis and oils, turning the meat to make sure it is evenly coated. Cover and refrigerate the bowl, and leave it to marinate for at least 2 hours, or overnight. Soak 12 wooden skewers in cold water for 1 hour, then thread four pork strips into an S-shape onto each skewer. Cover the skewers and refrigerate them until you are ready to start cooking.

Preheat the barbecue to medium direct heat. Toss the spring onions with the olive oil and season with salt and freshly ground black pepper. Cook on the flat plate for 10 minutes, or until softened and well browned. When the spring onions are nearly cooked, put the kebabs on the chargrill plate and grill them for 2 minutes on each side, or until the pork is just cooked through and glazed. Garnish the skewers with coriander sprigs. Serve immediately with the spring onion.

Notes Green ginger wine is a sweet, fortified wine with a distinctive ginger flavour; it originated in Britain. The best-known brands are Stone's and Crabbie's. This recipe is suitable for a flat or ridged grill plate.

Tuna steaks with salsa and mash

garlic mash

floury (starchy) potatoes	1 kg (2 lb 4 oz), cut into chunks
garlic cloves	6–8, peeled
milk	80 ml (3 fl oz/⅓ cup)
olive oil	60 ml (2 fl oz/¼ cup)

salsa

olive oil	1 tablespoon
French shallots	2, finely chopped
green olives	200 g (7 oz/1 heaped cup), pitted, quartered lengthways
currants	35 g (1 oz/¼ cup), soaked in warm water for 10 minutes
baby capers	1 tablespoon, rinsed and squeezed dry
sherry vinegar	1 tablespoon
mint leaves	2 tablespoons shredded

tuna steaks	4 (about 150 g/5 oz each)
olive oil	for brushing
sea salt	to taste

Boil the potato and garlic for 10–15 minutes, or until they are tender. Drain them, then return the pan to the heat, shaking it to evaporate any excess water. Remove the pan from the heat and mash the potato and garlic until they are smooth, then stir in the milk and olive oil, and season with salt and freshly ground black pepper.

To make the salsa, heat the oil in a frying pan over medium heat. Add the French shallots and cook for 2–4 minutes, or until they are softened, but not browned, then add the olives, drained currants and capers. Cook everything for 2 minutes, stirring it continuously, add the vinegar and cook for another 2 minutes, or until the liquid is reduced by about half. Remove the pan from the heat and keep the salsa warm until you're ready to dish up.

Preheat the chargrill plate to medium–high direct heat. Brush the tuna steaks with olive oil, season them well with sea salt and freshly ground black pepper, and grill for 2–3 minutes on each side for medium–rare, or until they are cooked to your liking. Stir the mint into the salsa and serve it immediately with the garlic mash and tuna.

Note Suitable for any barbecue.

Buffalo wings with ranch dressing

SERVES 4

chicken wings	12 large
garlic salt	2 teaspoons
onion powder	2 teaspoons
oil	for deep-frying
tomato sauce	125 ml (4 fl oz/½ cup)
Worcestershire sauce	2 tablespoons
butter	50 g (2 oz), melted
Tabasco sauce	to taste

ranch dressing

garlic clove	1 small, crushed
mayonnaise	185 g (7 oz/¾ cup)
buttermilk	125 ml (4 fl oz/½ cup)
flat-leaf (Italian) parsley	2 tablespoons finely chopped
chives	1 tablespoon finely chopped
lemon juice	1½ teaspoons
Dijon mustard	½ teaspoons
onion powder	1 teaspoon

Pat the wings dry with paper towels, remove and discard the tip of each wing, then cut them in half at the joint to create two pieces. Combine the garlic salt, onion powder and 2 teaspoons of ground black pepper, and rub the spice mixture into each chicken piece.

Deep-fry the chicken in batches for 2–3 minutes without letting it brown, then remove the pieces from the oil and drain them on crumpled paper towels. Once the chicken has cooled down a little, put it in a non-metallic bowl with the combined tomato sauce, Worcestershire sauce, butter and Tabasco, and toss so that all of the pieces are well coated in the marinade. Cover and refrigerate the bowl for at least 2 hours, or overnight.

To make the ranch dressing, mash the garlic and ¼ teaspoon salt to a paste then add the mayonnaise, buttermilk, parsley, chives, lemon juice, mustard and onion powder, and whisk it all together. Season well, cover and refrigerate for at least 1 hour before serving.

Preheat barbecue to medium direct heat. Cook the chicken for 6–8 minutes on each side, or until it is caramelized and sticky, turning and basting with the marinade as it cooks. Serve the chicken hot with the ranch dressing.

Note Suitable for a flat or ridged grill plate.

Barbecued corn in the husk

corn cobs	8 fresh young
olive oil	125 ml (2 fl oz/¼ cup)
garlic	6 cloves, chopped
flat-leaf (Italian) parsley	4 tablespoons chopped

Peel back the corn husks, leaving them intact. Pull off the white silks and discard. Wash the corn and pat dry with paper towels.

Combine the olive oil, garlic, parsley and some salt and black pepper and brush over each cob. Pull up the husks and tie together at the top with string. Steam over boiling water for 20 minutes, then pat dry.

Cook on a hot, lightly oiled barbecue grill or flatplate for 20 minutes, turning regularly. Spray with water during the cooking process to keep the corn moist.

Note Suitable for a flat or ridged grill plate.

desserts

It's time to round off the meal and tempt everyone with a mouthwatering dessert. Why go back into the kitchen? Make good use of the residual heat in your barbecue as it cools down to the perfect temperature after your main course. Clean off the grill and get mouths watering again with the scent of warm fruits and syrups wafting through the air. Just sit back and enjoy the compliments — there's no need to admit how easy it was! Apples, pears, bananas and stone fruits all lend themselves well to the barbecue treatment. Add lashings of cream or hot custard for a truly decadent result, and don't forget the marshmallows.

Grilled panettone with peaches

caster (superfine) sugar	125 g (5 oz/½ cup)
vanilla bean	½, halved and scraped
Grand Marnier	1 tablespoon
peaches	4 ripe
oil	for brushing
panettone	4 large slices
crème fraîche	80 g (3 oz/⅓ cup)

Put the sugar, vanilla bean and 60 ml (2 fl oz/¼ cup) water in a small saucepan and stir over low heat until the sugar has dissolved. Simmer the mixture, without stirring it, for 10 minutes, then remove it from the heat, stir in the Grand Marnier and keep it warm.

Dip the peaches into a saucepan of boiling water for 5 seconds then refresh under cold water and remove the skins, which should slip off easily. Cut the peaches in half, remove the stone and lightly brush the cut side with oil.

Preheat the chargrill plate to medium direct heat and grill the peaches, cut side down, for 5 minutes, or until they are golden and warmed through. Grill the panettone for 30 seconds to 1 minute on each side, or until it is marked and lightly toasted. The panettone will brown very quickly, so be careful to not burn it. Arrange the grilled peaches over the panettone, drizzle with the vanilla syrup and serve with a scoop of crème fraîche.

Note Suitable for any barbecue.

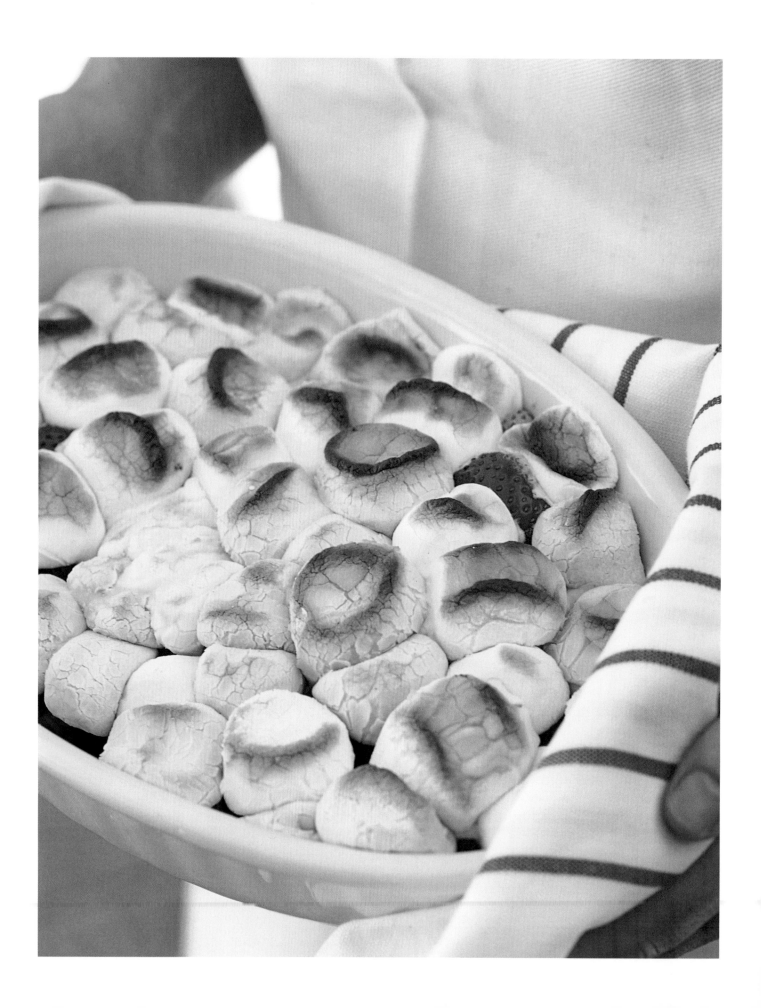

Berry and marshmallow gratin

mixed seasonal berries, such as strawberries, raspberries, blueberries, blackberries (see Notes)	600 g (1 lb 5 oz)
raspberry liqueur	2 tablespoons
pink and white marshmallows	150 g (5 oz/1²/₃ cups)
vanilla ice cream	to serve

Put the berries and raspberry liqueur in a bowl, stir gently to coat the berries and transfer them to a 1.5 litre (6 cup) ceramic ovenproof dish. Top the berries with the marshmallows, making sure they are evenly distributed over the surface.

Preheat a covered or kettle barbecue to medium–high indirect heat and put the dish in the middle of the barbecue. Let it cook for 8–10 minutes or until the berries are bubbling and the marshmallow has puffed up and is starting to melt. Serve the gratin immediately with a big scoop of ice cream, but take care to not burn your mouth on the berries, which will be very hot.

Note If it's not berry season, and your berries are not as sweet as they should be, add a little caster (superfine) sugar with the liqueur. Use strawberries in a smaller proportion to the other berries as they tend to release a lot of liquid. Suitable for a covered barbecue.

Fruit skewers with rum butter glaze

SERVES 4

peach	1, peeled, stoned and cut into 8 pieces
mango	1, peeled, stoned and cut into 8 pieces
strawberries	8, hulled and halved
papaya	160 g (6 oz), cut into 8 pieces
pineapple	160 g (6 oz) , cut into 8 pieces
bananas	2, cut into 2 cm (¾ inch) pieces
dark rum	185 ml (6 fl oz/¾ cup)
dark brown sugar	80 g (3 oz/⅓ cup)
butter	1 tablespoon
vanilla ice cream	to serve

Put the peach, mango, strawberries, papaya, pineapple and banana in a bowl with the rum and sugar, and stir gently until all of the fruit is coated in the marinade. Cover and refrigerate the bowl for 1 hour.

Soak eight wooden skewers in cold water for 1 hour. Drain the marinade into a small, heavy-based saucepan and thread the fruit onto the skewers. Make sure each skewer has a good mix of fruits and that the pieces are not crowded, or they won't cook evenly.

Bring the marinade to the boil over medium heat, then reduce the heat and simmer it for 5 minutes, or until it is reduced and syrupy. Remove the pan from the heat and whisk in the butter until it becomes smooth and glossy.

Preheat the flat grill plate to medium direct heat and cook the skewers for 5–8 minutes on each side, or until they are golden, basting them all over with the rum glaze during the last minute of cooking. Arrange the skewers on a serving plate, drizzle them with the rum glaze and serve warm with vanilla ice cream.

Note Suitable for a flat or ridged grill plate.

Coconut pancakes with grilled bananas

palm sugar or soft brown sugar	150 g (5 oz) roughly chopped
lime juice	2 tablespoons
plain (all-purpose) flour	125 g (5 oz/1 cup)
rice flour	45 g (1½ oz/¼ cup)
caster (superfine) sugar	125 g (5 oz/½ cup)
desiccated coconut	45 g (1½ oz/½ cup)
coconut milk	500 ml (17 fl oz/2 cups)
eggs	2, lightly beaten
bananas	4, sliced thickly on the diagonal
dark brown sugar	2 tablespoons
butter	50 g (2 oz), plus 20 g (1 oz) extra
shredded coconut	30 g (1 oz/½ cup), toasted
lime	1, cut into wedges

Put the palm sugar and 125 ml (4 fl oz/½ cup) water in a small, heavy-based saucepan and stir it over low heat for 5 minutes, or until the sugar has dissolved. Increase the heat to medium and let it simmer, without stirring, for 15 minutes, or until the liquid becomes a thick, sticky syrup. Stir in the lime juice and keep the syrup warm.

Sift the plain and rice flour together, add the caster sugar and desiccated coconut, and stir it all together. Make a well in the middle and pour in the combined coconut milk and egg, beating until the mixture is smooth.

Preheat the flat plate to low–medium direct heat. Toss the bananas in the brown sugar and grill them around the cooler edges of the flat plate, dotting each piece with butter. Cook the banana, turning occasionally, for 4–5 minutes, or until it begins to soften and brown. Melt a little of the extra butter in the middle of the plate and pour on 60 ml (2 fl oz/¼ cup) of the pancake mixture, using the back of a spoon to spread it out to a 15 cm (6 inch) circle. Cook the pancake for 2–3 minutes, or until the underside is golden, then turn it over and cook the other side for another minute. As each pancake is cooked, transfer it to a plate and cover it with a tea towel to keep it warm. Add more butter to the hot plate as necessary and keep going until all of the pancake mix has been used.

Fold each pancake into quarters and put two on each serving plate. Top them with grilled banana, drizzle each with a little palm sugar syrup, sprinkle with the coconut and serve with lime wedges.

Note Suitable for a flat grill plate.

Camembert with port-soaked raisins

SERVES 4

raisins	2 tablespoons
port	2 tablespoons
Camembert cheese	365 g (13 oz) whole
canola oil spray	for cooking
almond bread	to serve

Put the raisins and port in a small saucepan over high heat until they just come to the boil, then allow to cool for about 30 minutes.

Cut a circular lid from the top of the Camembert, leaving a 2 cm (¾ inch) border. Carefully remove the lid and scoop out the cheese with a teaspoon, leaving the base intact. Put the raisins in the hole and top with the cheese, squashing it down so that as much as possible fits back into the cavity, then replace the lid.

Spray a double layer of foil with canola oil spray and wrap the Camembert to form a sealed parcel. Preheat the flat plate to low direct heat and cook the parcel for 8–10 minutes, or until it is heated through and soft. Make sure the heat stays low, or the rind will go brown and burn. Serve with the almond bread.

Notes After cooking your main feast, there should be just enough heat left in the barbecue to warm the Camembert for this delicious dessert. Suitable for a flat or ridged grill plate.

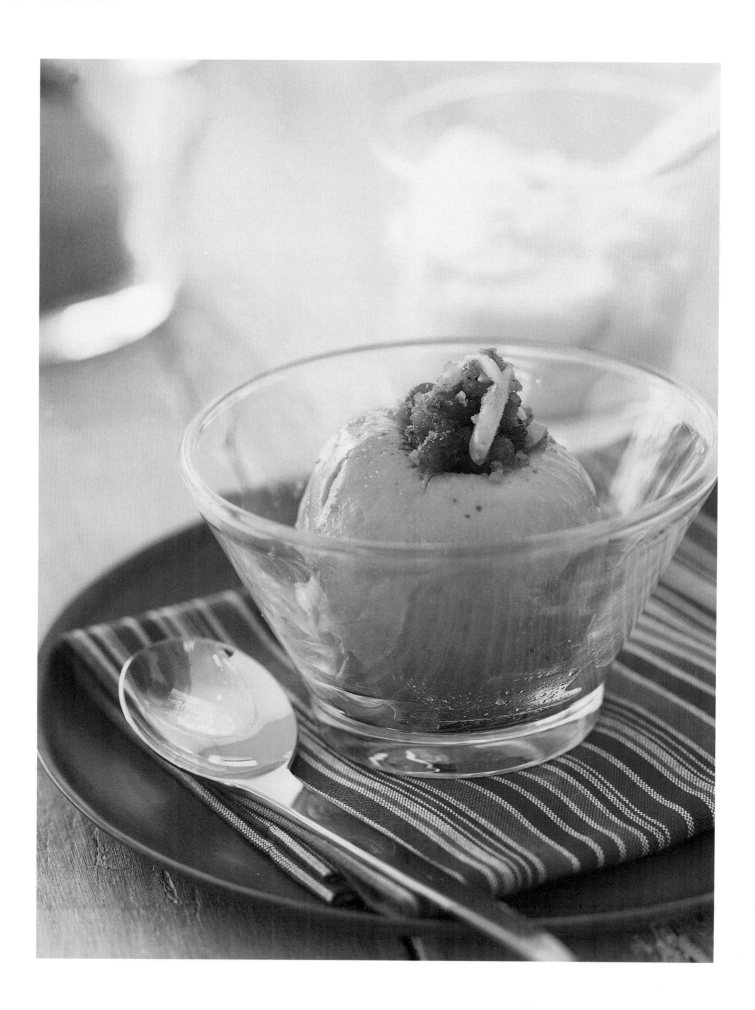

Amaretti-stuffed apples with ricotta

SERVES 4

sultanas	2 tablespoons
amaretto	2 tablespoons
amaretti biscuits	1o small (about 60 g/2 oz)
almonds	2 tablespoons slivered, toasted
sugar	1 tablespoon
butter	2½ tablespoons, melted
Granny Smith apples	4

vanilla ricotta

vanilla bean	½
icing (confectioners') sugar	2 tablespoons
ricotta cheese	250 g (9 oz/1 cup)

Soak the sultanas in the amaretto for 15 minutes or until they are softened, then add them to the crushed amaretti with the amaretto, almonds, sugar and 2 tablespoons of melted butter.

Scrape the seeds out of the vanilla bean and add them to the ricotta along with the icing sugar. Use an electric beater to beat the mixture until the ricotta is smooth and creamy.

Remove the apple cores and enough fruit from around the core to make a hole about 2.5 cm (1 inch) across. Stuff the hole with the amaretto mixture, brush the apples with the remaining melted butter and wrap them securely in foil. Preheat a kettle or covered barbecue to low–medium indirect heat, put the apples on the barbecue and cook, covered, for 15–20 minutes, or until tender. Serve with a big scoop of the vanilla ricotta.

Notes Vanilla ricotta is a delicious alternative to cream to serve with desserts. Suitable for a covered barbecue.

Pineapple with sugar glaze and coconut

SERVES 6

pineapple	1
dark brown sugar	115 g (4 oz/½ cup)
natural vanilla extract	½ teaspoon
Galliano	1 tablespoon
butter	60 g (2 oz)
coconut flakes	2 tablespoons, toasted
vanilla ice cream	to serve

Peel the pineapple and remove all the eyes, then slice it lengthways into quarters and remove the core. Cut the fruit into long 1 cm (½ inch) wide wedges.

Put the brown sugar, vanilla essence and 2 teaspoons water in a small saucepan and cook it over low–medium heat for 5 minutes, or until the sugar has dissolved. Remove the pan from the heat, add the Galliano, then return the pan to the heat and simmer the mixture for 3 minutes. Whisk in the butter and continue to simmer the mixture over low heat for 15 minutes, or until it is smooth and thick.

Preheat the chargrill plate to medium direct heat, brush the pineapple pieces with the brown sugar glaze, and grill them for 2–3 minutes, or until grill marks appear. Arrange the pineapple pieces on a serving platter, top them with the glaze and the toasted coconut, and serve with vanilla ice cream.

Note Suitable for any barbecue.

Pear and hazelnut crêpes with cinnamon

MAKES 12

crêpes

plain (all-purpose) flour	250 g (9 oz/2 cups)
eggs	3
milk	375 ml (13 fl oz/1½ cups)
butter	60 g (2 oz), melted, plus extra, for cooking

filling

cream cheese	500 g (1 lb 2 oz/2 cups)
icing (confectioners') sugar	2 tablespoons, sifted
hazelnuts	80 g (3 oz/⅔ cup), toasted, skinned and roughly chopped
candied peel	150 g (5 oz/⅔ cup)
lemon zest	2 teaspoons finely grated
Frangelico or Poire William	2 tablespoons
green pear	1 large firm, cored and cut into 1 cm (½ inch) dice
caster (superfine) sugar	2 tablespoons
ground cinnamon	1 teaspoon

To make the crêpe batter, sift the flour into a bowl with a pinch of salt and make a well in the centre. Gradually whisk in the combined eggs and milk until smooth, then stir in the melted butter. Strain the batter into a bowl, cover and refrigerate for 1 hour. The consistency should be similar to thin cream, so add a little more milk if it looks too thick.

To make the filling, beat the cream cheese and icing sugar in a bowl until smooth. Add the hazelnuts, candied peel, lemon zest and liqueur, and stir it all together. Gently stir in the diced pear and refrigerate the filling until you are ready to use it.

Heat an 18 cm (7 inch) crêpe or non-stick frying pan over low–medium heat and brush it with melted butter. Pour 60 ml (2 fl oz/¼ cup) of the batter into the pan, and swirl it around so that the bottom of the pan is thinly covered. Cook the crêpe for 1 minute or until the edges just begin to curl, then turn it over and cook the other side for 30 seconds. Slide the crêpe out of the pan onto a plate and continue with the remaining batter, stacking the crêpes as they cook.

Put 2 heaped tablespoons of the filling in the middle of each crêpe, fold two opposite sides in to the middle and flatten the mixture slightly, then fold in the other two sides to enclose the filling.

Preheat the flat plate to low direct heat and cook the crêpe parcels for 3–4 minutes on each side, or until they are golden and crisp, and the filling is warmed through. Transfer the parcels to serving plates, sprinkle them with the combined caster sugar and cinnamon, and serve them immediately.

Notes If you are making the crêpes in advance, stack them between sheets of greaseproof paper to stop them from sticking to each other. Do not refrigerate. Suitable for a flat grill plate.

Index

Published by Murdoch Books Pty Limited.

Murdoch Books Australia
Pier 8/9, 23 Hickson Road, Millers Point NSW 2000
Phone: +61 (0)2 8220 2000 Fax: +61 (0)2 8220 2558
www.murdochbooks.com.au

Murdoch Books UK Limited
Erico House, 6th Floor North, 93–99 Upper Richmond Road
Putney, London SW15 2TG
Phone: + 44 (0) 20 8785 5995 Fax: + 44 (0) 20 8785 5985
ww.murdochbooks.co.uk

Chief Executive: Juliet Rogers

Publisher: Lynn Lewis
Senior Designer: Heather Menzies
Editorial Coordinator: Liz Malcolm
Editor: Justine Harding
Designer: Katy Wall
Text and recipes: Tess Mallos
Additional recipes: Murdoch Books Test Kitchen
Photographers: Ashley Mackevicius, Prue Ruscoe and Ian Hofstetter; Martin Brigdale (location)
Stylists: Wendy Berecry, Jane Hann and Katy Holder
Food preparation: Ross Dobson and Georgina Leonard
Production: Kita George

National Library of Australia Cataloguing-in-Publication Data
Title: Barbecue.
ISBN 978-1-74196-954-2
Series: Food for Friends.
Notes. Includes index.
Subjects: Cookery, Barbecue.
641.76

Printed by 1010 Printing International Limited in 2010. PRINTED IN CHINA.

IMPORTANT: Those who might be at risk from the effects of salmonella poisoning (the elderly, pregnant women, young children and those suffering from immune deficiency diseases) should consult their doctor with any concerns about eating raw eggs.

CONVERSION GUIDE: You may find cooking times vary depending on the oven you are using. For fan-forced ovens, as a general rule, set the oven temperature to 20°C (70°F) lower than indicated in the recipe. We have used 20 ml (4 teaspoon) tablespoon measures. If you are using a 15 ml (3 teaspoon) tablespoon, for most recipes the difference will not be noticeable. However, for recipes using baking powder, gelatine, bicarbonate of soda, small amounts of flour and cornflour (cornstarch), add an extra teaspoon for each tablespoon specified.